Dark Psychology Mastery

Master the Secrets of Dark Psychology and Its Fundamentals Such as the Art of Reading People, Manipulation Techniques & How to Stop Being Manipulated, and Persuasion Skills!

By Pamela Hughes

Table of Contents

Introduction

Congratulations on purchasing Dark Psychology and thank you for doing so.

The following chapters will discuss everything that you need to know when it comes to persuasion, manipulation, Dark triad, and some case studies on dark psychology. There are a lot of manipulators, and individuals who are looking to get what they want, and they don't care whether they harm someone in the process of reaching their goals. They will use a lot of different techniques to get there, and often the victim doesn't even know what is going on. Even if they do catch on, they often feel so trapped in the cycle that it is hard to escape.

Manipulation is another form of mind control will be discussed in-depth in this guide book. Get to learn more about the techniques used for manipulation. If your aim is to influence a person and persuade them using the tactic of manipulation then this guide book will be of great help to you. Deception is also discussed in-depth. Deception is something that most people are familiar with although most people might not recognize it as a form of mind control.

A deeper understanding of these forms of mind control can assist to make it easier to be in control of your own mind and limit the influence that others have on your own. If you decide to take this path of persuasion to ensure that you do so with extreme caution, if applied maliciously it can be very dangerous and can get you into serious trouble. In this guide book, you will also learn the concept of the dark triad. The personality trait of Machiavellian, psychopathy, and narcissism in detail.

Chapter 1: The Concept of Dark Psychology

Dark psychology is the phenomenon by which people make use of techniques of coercion, motivation, manipulation, and persuasion to get what they desire or want. It is considered as human consciousness study and constructs of the human state as it associates to the psychological nature of humans to prey upon other humans, that is triggered by a psychopathic, psychopathological, or deviant criminal urge that lacks the general assumptions of instinctual urge, social sciences, and the theory of evolutionary biology.

Humanity has the power to victimize other living creatures and humans. While most people may sublimate or restrain this tendency. Dark psychology tends to understand the perceptions, thoughts, and feelings that lead to a person's predatory behavior. It is assumed that deviant and criminal abusive habits are purposive and have goal-oriented and rational motivation. Dark psychology suggests that there's a part within the human psyche that makes people behave in atrocious behaviors with no reason. Dark psychology suggests that every person has a reservoir of malevolent intention towards other people that ranges from minimally fleeting and obtrusive thoughts to total psychopathic deviant habits with no cohesive rationality. It is referred to as Dark Continuum.

Dark psychology isn't just about the dark part of your moon, but also the dark part of all the moons brought together. It consists of everything that makes you who you are in a relationship to your dark life. All faiths, humanity, and cultures have this proverbial cancer. From the time that you are born to the time you die, there's a part lurking within you that some people have referred to as evil, while other people have referred to it as the pathological, deviant, and criminal state. Dark psychology suggests that you have the ability for predatory habits and this ability has access to your perceptions, feelings, and thoughts. You have the potential but only a few people act upon their potential.

Every human being has had feelings and thoughts, at one point, of desiring to act in brutal behavior. At some point in life, you have had thoughts of harming others. If you're honest with yourself, you will agree that you have had the feelings and thoughts of desiring commit heinous acts. Having known that fact, you are a benevolent species: one would love to believe that you think these feelings and thoughts would not exist. Unfortunately, you have these thoughts, but you never act upon the thoughts.

Dark psychology suggests that there are people who have similar perceptions, thoughts, and feelings, but they act upon them in either impulsive or premeditated manner. The common difference is that they act upon their thoughts while other people have fleeting feelings and thoughts of doing so. If you believe in evolution, then you believe and know that every human behavior associated with the three main human instincts that include, instinctual urge to self-sustain, aggression, and sex.

Evolution adheres to the tenets of survival and the replication and fittest of the species. Every human being has a way to act in a manner to survive and procreate. Aggression manifests in you for the reasons of protecting your territory, marking your territory, and finally achieving the right to procreate. Your power of perception and thought has made you the apex of practicing brutality and apex of species. You will feel sorrow and cringe if you watch an antelope being ripped by a pride of lions. Though it is unfortunate and brutal, the main reason for the chaos fits the

11

evolutionary aspect of self-preservation. Lions hunt and kill for food, which is necessary for survival. Male creatures fight till death at times, for the will to power or rite of territory. These acts may seem brutal and violent, but evolution gives an explanation. Defiant people will tend to persecute other people, yet they will often consider themselves persecuted. Dark psychology will help you to be better prepared and reduce your chances of victimization by human predators.

The Six Tenets of Dark Psychology

Dark psychology is a universal aspect of the human state. Every society, culture, and people who live in them maintain this facet of the human state.

Better knowledge of the root cause and the triggers of dark psychology would appropriately enable the society to diagnose, reduce and recognize the dangers of its influence.

A better understanding of dark psychology has two-fold. First, having a better grasp of dark psychology of how it fits your original evolutionary reasons for struggling to survive. Secondly, by consenting that you have this potential for evil, allows you to reduce the probability of it erupting.

Due to its potential of being misinterpreted as psychopathy, dark psychology may be overlooked in its latent form. Modern psychology and psychiatry define psychopathy as a predator devoid of remorse for his/her action. It suggests that there is a continuum of severity ranging from feelings and thoughts to severe chaos and victimization with no reasonable motivation or purpose.

It assumes that every person has an ability for chaos. This ability is innate in every human and different external and internal factor increases the probability for this ability to show into violating behaviors. The behaviors are predatory in nature, and at some point, can act with no purpose. Psychology suggests that the predator-prey dynamic becomes distorted by human beings. It is specifically a human phenomenon and it is not shared by any other living creature. It is the study of human beings state that associates to a person's perceptions, thoughts, and feelings associated with this innate ability to prey upon other people devoid of definable purpose.

On the continuum, the intensity of dark psychology isn't deemed to be more or less heinous by the habit of victimization, but it maps out a range of inhumanity.

- **Dark Continuum**
  This is a very vital aspect to understand in your passage via your dark side and the dark side of humanity. It is an imaginary conceptual aspect that all sadistic, violent, criminal, and deviant behavior fall. It consists of perceptions, actions, feelings, and thoughts experienced by human beings. It ranges from severe to mild and from purposeless to purposive. A physical manifestation of dark psychology appears on the right side of the dark continuum and very extreme. Psychological manifestations of Dark psychology appear on the left side of the dark continuum, but it can be equally as destructive as physical acts.
- **Dark Factor**
  This is referred to as the place, realm, and potential that exists in every human being and is part of the human state. This aspect is one of the most abstract terms of dark psychology, this is because it's very direct to manifest through the written expression. The dark factor is a theoretical equation. It is a set of events that you experience, that increases your probability of engaging in predatory behavior. Research has it the children who are brought up in abusive households tend to become abusers

when they grow up, this doesn't mean that all abused children grow up to become violent offenders. This is just one facet of a multitude of circumstances and experiences that contribute to the Dark factor.

Dark psychology techniques that are often used on a daily basis. None of us desire to be a subject of manipulation and coercion, but it occurs often. You may not be the victim to another person specified in the dark triad, but normal, daily people like you experience dark psychology techniques on a daily basis.

These techniques are usually found in sales tactics, commercials, internet advertisements, even your manager's behaviors. When you have children, you will definitely face these techniques as your kids experiment with behaviors to get what they desire and seek autonomy. In fact, dark persuasion and covert manipulation are usually applied by people that you love and trust.

Below are some of the techniques applied often by normal, everyday people:

- **Bribery**
   The prominent psychologist B.F Skinner educated the universe about the power of reinforcement and shaping. Unfortunately, most people have applied it as a form of bribery. There is a difference between bribery and reinforcement. Reinforcement, if not properly managed can get perceived as bribery by the recipient and the relationship can fast turn into bribery expectations. This occurs when the other person says what they need you to do or give them in order to do an action.
- **Lying**

Exaggeration, lying, telling half-truths, and spinning the facts are probably the most popular manipulation techniques. You can normally spot lying by observing the body language of another person. The tells of lying consist of blushing, lack of eye contact, sweating, fidgeting, talking too much and contradictory body language.

Leading Questions

Leading questions is a dark psychology technique that applies a process of asking questions to set a standard and achieve a commitment. Once the person gets a level of commitment and enough yes replies, he/she will ask the subject for a commitment and appeal to the person's need to be consistent with his/her action and words.

This is the technique that is usually applied by unethical fundraisers. The presentation is a cycle of questions that get you to say yes as many times as possible, affirming the needs of the foundation, the needs of others, you need to assist, then the ultimate questions will be to ask for money.

This puts you in a position where when you say no, you fear being seen as not consistent with your affirmations, beliefs, and commitment.

Love Flooding

It occurs when a person offers you a great deal of love and affection. Touch, gifts, compliments, and attention are usually applied to flood you. The more you are in need of acceptance the not susceptible you are to this form of dark psychology. Once the manipulator creates a relationship with you and has created a dependency on their affection and love, they will then manipulate you by withdrawing their attention and love.

Love Withdrawal

It consists of withdrawing affection, attention, or love so that to get a specific behavior or response. This is a very dangerous technique if parents or guardians apply it with their kids. This technique is usually applied together with love flooding. However, the agent does not have to apply love flooding if they already have a bond with the victim.

Choice Restriction

It is when a person is attempting to get you to make a decision in compliance with their needs. Most salespersons are educated about this technique so that they can maximize their capacity for sales. This technique is seen during the closing stage of the sales pitch. It is often applied to a question.

The idea is to provide only two alternatives and distract you from an alternative option, that they would not want you to consider.

Passive-Aggressiveness

It seeks to avoid direct confrontation, yet seek to get a particular reaction. Passive-aggressive tactics include guilt inducement and sarcasm. Those who do not desire to be perceived as overly assertive or aggressive apply this technique. It is also applied by those who fear direct confrontation.

- **Subliminal Influence**

  It is a technique that applies auditory and visual stimuli to seed familiarity of a belief, service, product, or action. Subliminal messages appeal to the auditory and visual processing system of the mind. Your mind detects it and processes it, but at a subconscious point.

Videos that show a picture that you can't view has some influence on you, it is very small. Subliminal influence is very effective if applied as a subliminal prime.

This occurs when images or words are applied to get your brain more familiar with a particular idea. Later it is very probable that you will make a decision based on the image or word that you were primed with. Have you ever wondered how those magicians and mentalists are able to know what you are going to say or what person you will select? This is because they have seeded and primed your brain in a manner that you will revert to the priming idea or word. Most marketing techniques are based on this procedure.

- **Semantic manipulation**

    Applying words that are assumed to have a mutual or common meaning, yet the agent later tells you that he/she has a different understanding and meaning of the interaction. This is usually applied in interaction to create a sense of agreement by both parties, but the manipulator will later explain that his/her understanding of the words applied was different than the other party, thus excusing the breach of the agreement. Words are essential and powerful.

- **Reverse Psychology**

    It is a tactic involving the advocacy of a behavior or belief that is opposite to the one wanted, with the expectation that this procedure will encourage the victim of the persuasion to do what really is wanted that is opposite of what is suggested.

- **Mind Games**

    These are psychological tactics applied to generate a struggle between people for one-upmanship and psychological superiority. This tactic usually uses passive-aggressive behavior to particularly disempower or demoralize the thinking victim, making the aggressor look powerful. Mind games include communication techniques including social embarrassment and semantic manipulation.

Most people who use these dark psychology techniques know exactly what they are doing and they are intentional about manipulating you to getting what they desire, those who apply unethical and dark psychology techniques without being fully aware of it. Most of these people learned the techniques during childhood upbringing from their parents or guardian. Others learned the techniques in their adulthood or teenage years by happenstance. They applied a manipulation technique intentionally and it worked. They got what they desired. Therefore, they continue to apply the dark technique that assists them to get what they want anytime.

In other instances, people are trained to apply these dark psychology techniques. Training programs that teach persuasion technique, unethical, dark psychological techniques are normally marketing or sales programs. Most of these programs apply dark techniques to sell a product or generate a brand with the aim of serving themselves or their company not their customers.

Who Apply Dark Psychology?

Sociopaths

Those who are truly sociopathic; meeting clinical diagnosis, are usually intelligent, charming, yet impulsive. Due to inadequate emotionality and capability to feel remorse, they apply dark psychology techniques to create a superficial bond and then take advantage of others.

Politicians

Most politicians apply dark psychology techniques and dark persuasion techniques to convince people they are right and get votes.

Narcissists

Those who are truly narcissistic, have an inflated sense of self-worth. They require other people to validate their belief in being powerful. They have dreams of being adored and worshipped. They apply dark techniques, manipulation, and dark persuasion to maintain this.

Attorneys

Most attorneys concentrate so intently on winning their cases that they resort to applying unethical persuasion techniques to get the result they desire.

Public Speakers

Most speakers apply unethical techniques to heighten the emotional condition of the audience knowing very well it leads to selling more products at the back of the room.

Salespeople

Most salespersons get so concentrated on attaining a sale that they resort to unethical techniques to persuade and motivate people to purchase their products.

Leaders

Most leaders apply unethical techniques to get higher performance, get compliance or greater effort from their subordinates.

Selfish People

This can be any person who has an agenda of self before other people. They will apply techniques to attain their own needs first, even someone else's expense. They do not mind win-lose results.

Chapter 2: Covert Emotional Manipulation

Manipulation is a kind of social influence that targets to alter the perception or behavior of other people via underhanded tactics, deceptive or indirect tactics. By advancing the desires of the manipulator always at other people's expense, such methods could be considered devious and exploitative. The manipulator will deliberately build an imbalance of power, and he/she will exploit the victim to serve their purpose.

Emotional manipulation refers to a manner by which a person who is wise influences you to respond or behave to situations and issues in a manner that is unoriginal to yourself but which fits their purpose. The aspect isn't usually forceful but has to do with playing with your emotions or mind to exploit you.

It relates to someone using what belongs to you in a covert way to feed their own desires without getting your consent. The main issue is not about the manipulators acting in secrecy, but most of them make you do things you wouldn't ideally have done, maybe even an act you consider bad or you seriously object to.

Why You Need to Know Emotional Manipulation Tactics

If you are ignorant of the tactics applied to you by the manipulators, you will not be able to break loose from their spell. You will always deceive yourself that you are in charge of your life when you are really not in charge of your life. When you have the ability to identify the tactics used by the manipulators, you can easily identify when they are being used on you.

At times most people would say that emotional manipulation is a bad habit, there may be specific times that you will need to apply it when you want to get what you desire from people who may initially not have cooperated with you. An understanding of the techniques would guide you in knowing what to do in such situations. Emotional manipulators work on the victim's psychological weak points.

Characteristics of Emotional Manipulators

Domineering

Secrecy. They tend to work behind the scenes for them to achieve their desire. Although when the manipulators have gotten you on their grasp they tend to come to the open and brag about it good listeners. They pay close attention to the details of your interactions with them, and from that, they are able to pick where to start controlling you.

Deception. That has the ability to make you see a black thing as white using cunningness or craft.

Emotional Manipulation Techniques

Gaslighting

To gaslight, a person is to cause them to doubt something about themselves that is real. Though in a covert way, they tend to ask questions that would make think twice about even the things you have often held to be sacrosanct.

For you to combat this emotional technique, you need to document your experiences and life happenings and you should often refer to them. This will help you not to doubt even a single of your experiences.

Denial

It's very hard to separate denial, lying and the distortion of facts from emotional manipulation. Although a manipulator may not often be opposed to the fact, their supposed acceptance of it is to serve their purpose to manipulate you later on. They will consent to a fact only to deny it later on.

Projection

Manipulators use this tactic to shift their shortcomings or deficiencies to another person. Instead of them taking responsibility for their errors, they would rather place the blame on someone else. It is an abusive technique that seeks to take the burden of guilt from them to another person. Their main purpose is to paint themselves clean while the other person looks unfortunate and dirty.

They aim to make you look weak while they appear to be strong. You should check out for people who easily notice wrongs in others: they are only projecting their negative selves.

Intimidation

When a manipulator considers you to be a threat, he/she tend to silence you. They tend to stay close to you and talk in a manner that combines subtlety and aggressiveness. Manipulators will tend to look into your eyes with strange body language so that you can forget your train of thought or end an interaction with them.

To combat this technique, you need to get over your fears and learn to stand up to intimidation. As a precautionary move, you should prevent yourself from revealing your weaknesses or fears to someone you cannot trust. Ask for help from other people where and when you need it but you should never make the manipulators feel that you are afraid of anything, even them.

Magnify their own problems while diminishing yours. They pretend that they are so sorry for what you are going through and they would also put on a show of short-lived empathy, this is to hide their true intentions. However, they will quickly bring up their difficulties too and magnifying them so that yours look insignificant.

Intellectual Bullying

They will tend to overwhelm you will intellectual facts. They may not be so accurate, but they know that you do not have the chance or access to verify the authenticity of their claims. To an extent, manipulators place themselves before you as an authority of some kind so as to have their way with you.

To combat this tactic, you need to inform. You do not have to know everything about everything, but endeavor to know something about everything. When a person approaches you with an alleged fact, apart from you not being swept off your feet, you are able to correctly predict its authenticity or not.

Intentional Digression

It refers to deviating from the normal course of interaction to something completely irrelevant to the issue at hand.

Name-calling

A major characteristic of an emotional manipulator is that they have an exalted but always false opinion of themselves. They tend to be often right while everyone else is often wrong. Most of the people who practice emotional manipulation tend to be narcissists. So, when you try to challenge their ego, be prepared to get some more names in addition to those on your birth certificate.

To combat this technique, you should state frankly to them that you take exception to them calling you names.

Stalking and Gossiping

The main purpose of manipulation is to create Byron you. But when it seems controlling you might be very difficult, they can change their technique to controlling how people see or view you. Manipulators seek to achieve this by them spreading falsehood about you behind your back. In some situations, they may even be forced to stalk you: that is monitoring you around. The main reason is to intimidate and give people a bad impression of you.

Conditioning

This is a psychological method of training a person towards a specific taste or trait that the trainer wants. The purpose is to make you get rid of your initial values and embrace those of the manipulators.

How You Can Manipulate People (Techniques)

Every single tactic you need so that you can manipulate the minds of others. Always try to be smart about using the tactics, practice a lot and soon you will be able to influence how other people behave and think.

Fear and relief tactic. This technique involves playing a bit with someone's emotions and while it's a fact that this tactic can cause a great deal of anxiety and stress, this tactic is very efficient.

This technique had two parts: First, you should make another person fear something. By doing so, you will make the other person vulnerable to the illogical behavior that you can use for your advantage. Secondly, you offer the person relief of the fear that he/she is experiencing.

Mirroring Tactic

This technique involves two parts. First, when you are trying to mirror the person you are trying to manipulate and secondly, the person you are trying to manipulate will be mirroring you. Mirroring establishes trust between you and the other person and it also helps you create a connection that you will finally begin to exploit. The tactic is quite simple all that you need to do is to copy the behavior. Always take a close look at the person's body language, hand and face gestures and the tone of their voice.

Guilty Approach

Do not underestimate the potential of making a person feel guilty about something. If a person tends to feel guilty about something, he/she will do anything possible to compensate for it. At this point, is when you start planting your own ideas into someone's subconscious mind and wait for them to flow with it.

Playing the Victim Card

This tactic goes hand in hand with the guilty approach technique, you should consider combining the two do you to achieve the best outcome. But remember to be more careful when you are using the playing victim technique because at times it can be a double-edged sword and it can work against you if you overdo it.

You pretend to be the victim in a situation, making others feel sorry for you and make them feel bad about how they are treating you. This occurs by allowing your targets to feel like they are the one trying to influence you.

Bribery Technique

This tactic is widely used and it often works like a charm whenever you try to make someone do what you desire. When you reward someone, they will feel compelled to return the favor. Always make sure to use it in your best interest when they return the favor. Try and figure out what your significant other needs and just give it to them, make sure that you suggest something in return. Always be careful that it does not sound that you are blackmailing them, as that may not end up well.

Love Bombing Tactic.

This tactic is used at the start of an interaction with the person you are trying to influence, you demonstrate positive attention and affection towards your target and it will be very challenging afterward for them not to feel good about you. Naturally, it is a person's instinct to treat people nicely if they do the same.

If you begin an interaction with being very nice towards a person, you are setting up an emotional trap for them, and they will likely fall into the trap.

Be a Good Listener

Developing trust between you and the other person is a very important aspect of influence. If someone does not trust you, he/she will not want to interact with you and you will lose the opportunity of influencing them. That is why it is very vital to actually be friends and one of the best ways to do so is by you being a good listener.

Benefits of Being a Good Listener:

- **Creates an illusion of friendliness at the prices of the interaction.**

  You will seem to be trustworthy and appealing when people see that you are interested in what they have to say. It strengthens your trust when you after some time mention what they had told you before. This shows that you actually cared and genuinely listened to them.

- **Learn to interpret body language.**

  Most people will tend to express themselves more through their body language than their real words. When you find it challenging to decipher a person, what you have to do is to pay close attention to their body language.

  For you to effortlessly influence a person, you must figure out the person's emotional and psychological makeup, and you can't do that without taking their body language into consideration.

- **Make use of your looks in your best interest.**

  Whether you like it or not, human nature is very shallow to a specific extent, you are naturally attracted to charismatic people. If you are a good-looking person, you can make the best out of it and influence others. You have to be cheerful, positive and have an approachable and welcoming body language. Make people feel very special and ensure that you are often confident about yourself.

Developing Skills

You need to have great verbal communication skills for you to be able to manipulate people. Being able to speak clearly and expressing your thoughts skillfully is very vital.

Enhancing verbal communication for better manipulation

Begin reading as much as you can. It is very key to have a broader vocabulary and reading is the proper way to enhance it.

Avoid simple texts that even a fifth-grader can handle. Apart from vocabulary, reading will expand your knowledge about various topics.

- **Always practice your speaking in front of a mirror.**

    It's important for you to see and observe the manner in which you speak and get comfortable with it. In that process of observing yourself, you will be able to find details that you don't like and you will change it. If you do not like the details neither will other people.

- **Work on your tone and voice.**

    What you say is not only a vital thing. How you do it isn't any less important. Record your voice, listen to it, and analyze the details. Write down what you like about it and what you do not like about it. Working on your voice will increase your success rate of mental manipulation. Do not speak quietly and monotonously. Ensure that everything that you utter is clear and with confidence. Ensure that you look good in front of the people you want to influence.

Protecting Yourself from Manipulation

All emotions, bad or good, they serve a purpose in your life - but always be aware of those people who want to use the power of emotions to influence or manipulate you. If you are identified as an empath, this will particularly apply to you, as this type of person will be most vulnerable to picking up negative energy from other people.

Tips to safeguard yourself from the emotional situation:
Do not fall into their trap. People who have pleasure in toying with other people's emotions will use any kind of techniques such as interrogation, confusion, and blame, in order to really get into your nerves. If you have to deal with this kind of people, just ignore them or surprise them by uttering something nice instead

of meeting them with a combative attitude. Manipulators thrive off getting a rise out of you, ensure that you do not give them what they desire.

Begin writing down what the manipulators say during interactions.

They have a bit of making you look like the bad person, and twisting their words to suit their agenda. For you to make sure that you can actually show them what they said in earlier interactions, write down any details you think they might conveniently alter later in order to justify their behavior. Manipulators may try to convince you that they never said a particular thing, but you can prove them wrong with your notes. Be smart about safeguarding yourself from the manipulator's wrath, and they may soon get discouraged from using you as their emotional toys.

- **Call them out on their behavior**.

    Manipulators have often bossed others around for a long period and they have never been confronted for it. Always stand up for yourself and let them know that they make you feel uncomfortable and taken advantage of.

    Stay away whenever possible. Avoiding emotional instigators and manipulators will probably eliminate your chances of being taken advantage of by manipulators. For you to achieve this, ensure that you read people's energy when you first meet them. When you do not get a proper vibe from them, simply trust your gut, and make a decision to stay away from them.

- **Avoid emotional attachment**.

    Particularly manipulators do not show their true colors immediately. Pay close attention to the first sign of them fully steamrolling your emotions, slowly back away from the relationship, and ensure that you let them know your boundaries. They constantly scan the horizon for their next target, but it will be much easier to break away if you have not invested so much in the relationship to start with. If it's a must that you interact with them, ensure that you keep it cordial, civil relationship, but do not let it go any further than that if you really value your emotional well-being.

- **Meditate always.**

For you to ensure that you keep your vibration high, you require to silence your mind, breathe deeply, and get in touch with the higher realms to adequately handle yourself on Earth. This will assist you to deal with manipulators appropriately, this is because you will have inner peace no matter how much chaos happens around you. Meditation will allow you to cultivate compassion for this person and open your eyes to what they have been through in life. Always meet hostility with understanding and love, and you might witness them transforming into a new person.

- **Tell them "you are right".**

As it might be hard for the ego, your soul will give you a round of applause. Manipulators feed on drama, so when you agree with them you will leave them speechless and fast put out the flames of their delusions. For the sake of your peace of mind simply let manipulators win the argument. Knowing deep down that their behavior and accusations are wrong, but they will have to deal with that karma later on.

- **Inspire them.**

It is very vital to be the change, and in this case, it will protect you because manipulators will not emit negative vibes against you after they are inspired by your own positive actions, non-manipulative actions. You should bring up the advantages of meditation, taking responsibility for their own life, volunteering, exercising, following their trues passions and eating a clean diet. Make use of the knowledge that you have about becoming your best self in order to assist them to become their best self too.

- **Let go of harmful Ties.**

When you notice such behavior in your spouse, boyfriend, or girlfriend, you should leave that relationship for your own well-being. You cannot force someone to change, no matter how many times you have brought up their volatile behavior. You deserve a person who will balance and nurture your emotions, not a person who desires to use you for their own personal fulfillment.

- **Have positive self-talk.**

Manipulators can actually tarnish your otherwise peppy mood, so ensure that you restore yourself with positive uplifting affirmations during the day. Manipulators thrive on seeing you your mood go down the drain, so when they observe that you are unaffected by their remarks, they will not have a reason to torment you ever again.

- **Develop a strong mentality.**

Do not ever let their outbursts or insults ever get into your mind: entertain their thought or even laugh at them without consenting to them. If you know what type of person you are and have a strong sense of self-worth nothing that they say will ever bring you down.

Chapter 3: Dark Triad

Most people have traits that make it difficult or disagreeable to deal with or associate with them. These kinds of people tend to be domineering, arrogant or volatile, but, with careful understanding and management, you can develop the strengths to neutralize the unsavory or negative elements of their behavior, and restore peace.

But there are some characteristics and behaviors that can be so damaging and, if a person exhibits a toxic combination of these traits, he/she can undermine his/her colleagues in a lasting manner, he/she can potentially destroy or poison a group or team.

What is Dark Triad?

The dark triad is a term that refers to the three distinct but related personality traits: psychopathy, narcissism, and Machiavellianism.

Psychopathy Background

So as to clear up any misconception about the definitions of psychopath and sociopath. In the early 1800s, medical practitioners who dealt with mental patients start to realize that some of the patients who were outwardly normal had what the doctors referred to as moral insanity or moral depravity in that the patients seemed to have no sense of rights or ethics to other people. Psychopathy was first used for this kind of people around 1900. The word was altered to the sociopath into the 1930s to emphasize the harm they cause to society.

Characteristic of a Psychopath and Psychopathic Traits

There are various characteristics and traits of psychopaths. While psychopaths are individuals, psychopaths share many aspects of their personality. The Hare Psychopath Checklist-Revised (PCL-R) draws twenty characteristics of a psychopath grouped into four proved factors.

Emotional or Affective Characteristics of a Psychopath

Emotions of a psychopath have particular traits. One emotional characteristic is the inadequacy of guilt or remorse. This psychopath's emotional characteristic explains why psychopathic murderers can commit heinous acts, for example, murder and not feel bad about the heinous acts. Affective characteristics include:

- Failure to accept responsibility for their own acts
- Have shallow emotions, that is, their emotions may be felt but is fleeting and shallow manner.
- Callousness and lack of empathy
- Antisocial Traits

These are traits that go against society's conventions. For instance, early behavioral and juvenile delinquency problems are antisocial traits that most psychopaths possess. Other antisocial traits include:

- Criminal versatility
- Poor Behavior controls
- Revocation of conditional release

Lifestyle Traits

Not only can their traits be seen in the interpersonal aspects and emotions but can be experienced in the lifestyle as well. An example of this trait is where the psychopath uses a parasitic lifestyle where he/she feeds off the others. He/she achieve this by utilizing interpersonal traits.

Some lifestyle traits include:

- Irresponsibility
- Inadequacy of realistic long-term desires
- Impulsivity

Interpersonal Traits

The most common interpersonal trait is pathological lying. They constantly lie to hide their psychopathic traits and anti-social behaviors that are illegal.

Other interpersonal traits include:

- Being manipulative and conning
- Superficial charm and glibness
- Grandiose sense of self-worth

Narcissism

Such people manifest a long term and pervasive pattern of an excessive sense of self-importance, complete lack of empathy towards others, and extreme preoccupation with themselves. Such a person feels entitled to power, and prestige became their distorted thought pattern gives him/her an overblown sense of superiority. The distorted thought patterns and related behaviors can be linked back to adolescence.

Those who have this personality see themselves and their opinions and interest as the only things that really matter. Narcissists have no ability for empathy and can't associate or appreciate feelings outside their feelings, this makes treatment of narcissistic personality close to impossible.

The exaggerated sense of self-importance and arrogance may look like self-confidence, but most people with this kind of personality have exceedingly fragile self-esteem. This gives an explanation of the insatiable need for unreasonable expectations and admiration of favorable treatment from other people. When other people fawn and admire over them, it feeds the narcissist's self-esteem.

People with this personality trait usually exaggerate talents and accomplishments. When their lies are discovered, they may lash out or attempt to get revenge by spreading cruel rumors about the inferior people.

Causes of Narcissistic personality

Experts do not have a clear understanding of the cause of this personality trait. Researchers theorize that a genetic predisposition contributes to the development of this personality, but that genes alone do not cause the onset of the personality. Most people believe that early childhood upbringing, for example, overbearing parenting and excessive insensitive parenting, play part in the development of this personality.

Other risk factors:

- Being male
- Observing caregivers manipulate others to meet their emotional and physical desires.
- Extreme emotional abuse during upbringing
- Experiencing unpredictable parental care

- Receiving excessive criticism for bad behavior throughout childhood
- Receiving profound neglect or admiration by one or both parents

Signs of Narcissism Personality

These are behaviors that you can see in a person through simple observation:

Sense of entitlement scenario. People with narcissistic personality traits may have:

- Excessive sensitivity to rejection.
- An attraction to leadership position or high-profile professions.
- A pattern of rapidly alternating between devaluation and idealization of other people.
- An unstable self-perception that is between excessive self-hate and self-praise.
- An overwhelming desire to be the center of attention and admiration.
- A history of intense but short relationships.
- A scale in which they rate other people in terms of usefulness.
- Interpersonally exploitive scenario.
- Grandiosity scenario.
- Symptoms of Narcissistic personality.
- They appear in adolescence or later than adulthood. They make up a large part of the person's inexperience.

The traits include:

- Demonstration of haughty and arrogant behaviors
- Lack of empathy
- Need for excessive admiration

- Envy of other people or the belief that other people envy him/her
- Sense of entitlement
- Grandiose sense of self-importance.

Machiavellianism

It refers to a personality trait which sees a person so concentrated on their own interests they will deceive, manipulate, and exploit other people to accomplish their desires.

It involves deceit and manipulative, cynical opinion towards human nature, and a calculating and cold attitude towards other people.

A person with this kind of trait will tend to have the following tendencies:
- Lack of warmth in social gatherings.
- Rarely reveal their real intentions.
- Might struggle to identify their own feelings.
- Prone to casual sex encounters.
- Can be quite patient because of their calculating nature.
- Not often aware of the outcomes of their actions.
- Low levels of empathy.
- Deceive and lie when needed.
- Use flattery usually.
- Usually, avoid emotional attachments and commitments.
- Have the ability to cause harm to other people in order to accomplish their goal.
- Cynical of morality and goodness.
- Come across as confident and charming.
- Come across as hard to get to know or aloof.
- Lacking in values and principles.
- Are good at analyzing social events.

- Manipulate and exploit other people to get ahead.
- They prioritize power and money over relationships.
- They only concentrate on their own interests and ambitions.

Chapter 4: Deception

Deception is one of the forms of mind control. This kind of mind control has some similarities to manipulation in the fact that manipulators will apply a lot of deception in order to get their final desire.

What is Deception?

Deception, along with deceit, beguilement, subterfuge, bluff, and mystification, is an act applied by the manipulator to propagate beliefs in the victim about things that are falsehood or those that are a partial truth.

Deception may involve a lot of different things, for example, dissimulation, distraction, camouflage, sleight hand, and concealment. The manipulator will be able to control the mind of the victim because the victim is going to believe and trust them. The victim will believe what the manipulator wants to continue on with their victim.

Deception will always come up in terms of relationship and it can lead to emotions of betrayal and distrust between the two spouse who is in the relationship. This is because deception violates the rules of many relationships and is also seen to have a negative impact on the expectations that come with that relationship. Many people expect to be able to have a truthful interaction with their partner: if they learn that their partner is deceptive, they would have to learn and understand how to use distraction and misdirection in order to get the truthful and reliable information that they need.

Types of Deception

This is a form of communication that depends on lies and omissions in order to convince the victim of the world that best fits the manipulator. Since there is communication included, there will also be various types of deception that could be happening.

There are five types of deception. Some of these types of deception have been manifested in the other forms of mind control, manifesting that there can be some overlapping.

These five types of deception include:

Concealment

Concealment is one of the most popular types of deception. Concealment is when the manipulator omits information that is very key to the context, intentionally or the manipulator engages in any behavior that would tend to hide information that is key to the victim for that specific context. The manipulator won't have directly lied to the victim, but the manipulator will have made sure that the key information that is required never makes it to the victim.

Lies

This is when the manipulator makes up information that is fully different from what is the fact. The agent will present this information to the victim as fact and the victim will view it as the truth. This can be very dangerous since the victim will not realize that he/she is being lied to or fed false information: if the victim knew the information was no true, the victim will not likely be talking to the manipulator and no deception will happen.

Exaggeration

Exaggeration is when the manipulator will stretch the truth or overstate a fact a little bit in order to turn the story the way they would desire. While the manipulator may not be directly lying to the victim, the manipulator is going to make the situation seem like a bigger deal than it actually is or the manipulator may alter the fact a little bit so that the victim will perform what he/she desires.

Equivocations

Equivocation is when the manipulator will make an indirect statement, ambiguous or contradictory statements. Equivocation is done to lead the victim to get confused and do not understand what is happening. Equivocation can also assist the manipulator to save face if the victim comes back and tries to blame the manipulator for the false information.

Understatements

This is the exact opposite of exaggeration tool in that the manipulator is going to minimize or downplay aspects of the truth. The manipulator will tell the victim that a situation is not that big of a deal when the truth is that it could be the thing that determines if the victim will graduate or get the promotion. The manipulator will be able to go back later and say how he/she did not realize how big of a deal it was, leaving the manipulator looks good and the victim to look almost petty if the victim complains.

The agent of deception is going to use any technique that is at their disposal in order to get their desired goal, much like what happens in the other forms of mind control.

Motives for Deception

There are three main motives that are present in deception found in close ties. These motives include:

Partner Focused Motives

In this type of motive, the manipulator is going to apply deception in order to avoid causing harm to the victim, or their partner. The manipulator may also apply deception in order to protect the victim's relationship with an outside third party, to avoid having the victim worrying about something, or to keep the self-esteem of the victim intact. This kind of motivation is viewed as socially polite as well as relationally beneficial.

Self-Focused Motive

This motive is not considered to be as noble as the first one and is, therefore, more looked down upon than the other techniques. Rather than worrying about the victims and how they are feeling, the manipulator is going to just think about how they feel and about their own self-image. In this motive, the manipulator uses deception in order to enhance and protect their self-image. This kind of deception is applied in order to shield the manipulator from anger, criticism, or embarrassment.

When this kind of deception is applied in a relationship, it's often perceived to be a more serious issue and transgression than what is found with the partner-focused deception. This is because the manipulator chooses to act in a selfish way rather than working to protect the relationship or the partner.

Relationship Focused Motive

This deception is applied by the manipulator in the hope of limiting any harm that might come to the relationship simply by avoiding relational conflict and trauma. Depending on the situation, this form of deception will sometimes assist the relationship and at other times it might be the cause of harming the relationship because it's going to make things very complicated. For example, when you decide to hide how you are feeling about supper because you do not want to get in conflict this might assist the relationship. Contrary, if you had an affair and decide to keep this information to yourself, it is only going to make things very complicated than it was ultimately.

Regardless of the intent of deception in a relationship, deception is not recommended at all. The manipulator is withholding information that might be very key to the victim: once the victim finds out about the situation, the victim will begin to lose trust in the agent and wonder what else the manipulator is hiding from him/her. The victim isn't going to be very concerned for the reason behind the deception, the victim will just be upset that something has been kept from him/her and the relationship will start having cracks. It's good for you to stick to the policy of honesty in the relationship and surround yourself with people who don't practice deception in your social gathering.

Detecting Deception

If a victim is interested in avoiding deception in their life, in order to avoid the mind games that come along with the deception. It is always a good idea to first learn how to detect when deception is happening. Often, it is very challenging for the victim to determine that deception is happening unless the manipulator slips up and either tells a lie that is blatant or obvious or he/she contradicts something that the victim already knows to be a fact. While it may be very hard for the manipulator to deceive the victim for a long period of time, it is something that will normally happen in everyday life between people who know each other well. Detecting when deception happens is always very hard because there is not enough indicator that is fully reliable to tell when deception occurs.

Though deception is capable of placing a large load on the cognitive functioning of the victim since the victim is going to have to figure out how to remember all the statements that he/she has made to the victim so that the story remains consistent and believable. Just one slip up and the victim will be able to tell that something is not okay. Due to the strain of keeping the story straight, the manipulator is likely to leak out information to tip off the victim either through verbal or nonverbal cues.

Detecting deception is believed to process that is cognitive, complex, and fluid and which will always vary depending on the message that is being exchanged. Deception is a dynamic and iterative process of influence between the manipulator, who works to manipulate the information how he/she desires it so that it varies from the truth, and the victim, who will try to figure out if the information is valid or invalid. The manipulator's actions are going to be interrelated to the actions that the victim takes after he/she receives the information. During this exchange, the manipulator is going to reveal the verbal and nonverbal information that will cue the victim into the deceit. At some particular point, the victim may be able to tell that the manipulator has been lying to him/her.

When deception happens, it needs a conscious behavior that is deliberate on the part of the manipulator so listening to words and paying close attention to the body expression that is going on is both vital when attempting to determining if someone is deceiving you.

Basically, there are no many signs that can be considered when attempting to figure out when deception is happening.

Components of Deception

While it may be very hard to determine which factors show when deception is happening, there are some elements that are typical of deception. The victim will always not realize that these elements have happened unless the manipulator has been caught in the act of deceiving or told an outright lie.

Components of Deception include:

Simulation

Simulation involves showing the victim information which is not true. There are techniques that are applied when it comes to simulation, these include mimicry, distraction, and fabrication.

Mimicry, or copying prof another model, the manipulator will be unconsciously depicting something that is same to himself/herself. The agent may have an idea that is similar to someone else and instead of giving credit, the agent will say that it's all his/hers. This type of simulation always happens through visual, auditory, and other means.

Distraction:

This is when the manipulator attempts to get the victims to concentrate their attention on something other than the truth: often by baiting or offering something that might be more tempting than the truth that is being hidden. For example, if the husband is cheating and he thinks that the wife is beginning to know, the husband may bring home a pretty dress to distract the wife form the issue for a short while. The issue with this method is that it doesn't last for long and the manipulator must find another way to deceive the victim do them to keep the process moving.

Fabrication:

This is another tool that a manipulator may use when deceiving. The manipulator takes something that is found in reality and alters it so that it varies. The manipulator may tell a story that didn't occur or add embellishments that make it sound worse or better than it was.

Research on Deception

Deception has become part of your daily life. Whether the manipulator means not to cause harm or vice versa, there are many instances where deception will creep into a relationship of all kinds. The manipulator may deceive their boss for them to get more time to complete a particular task: a spouse man deceives a partner in order not to hurt their feelings. Due to this prevalence, there has been some research to try and determine why it happens and who may be more likely to perform deception.

These researches include:

Psychological Research

This branch will use deception the most because this is necessary to determine the outcomes that would really happen. The rationale behind doing this deception states that humans are very sensitive to the way that they might appear to others, as well as to themselves, and the self-consciousness that they feel may distort or interfere with the way the victim would believe in normal situations outside of doing the research where they would not feel scrutinized.

Spotting a Deceptive Behavior and Lies

When the verbal aspect and the visual aspect of a message do not align, then you are doomed. Here are some tips that will show you when a person is telling a lie:

- Building rapport. Good cops normally get better outcomes compared to bad cops. Come across as empathetic in an interaction, and you will get someone to open up more than when you are accusatory and cold.

- Surprise them. A deceptive person will always attempt to anticipate your questions, this is to ensure that their replies sound natural and instinctive. A deceptive person may even practice replying to particular questions ahead of time. Try and ask them something that they do not expect and for sure they will stumble.

- Learn to listen more than you speak. Liars will tend to speak more compared to truthful people in an attempt to sound legitimate and win over the target audience. Liars will use a more complex sentence to hide the facts.

You should be wary of the following:

Repetitive clearing the throat and coughing are signs of tension.

People who are so stressed tend to talk louder. When a person crack in their natural tone of voice often occurs at the point of deception.

Stressed People Often Speak Faster

This is not to assume that an interaction with your partner who does the above is lying to you. But if you witness the above behavior please you should proceed with caution. Pay attention to behavior change. A subtle alteration in someone's deportment can be a strong sign of deception.

You should be careful if a person:

- Keep using extreme exaggerated or superlatives replies, for example, when some respond everything is 'brilliant' or 'awesome' instead of a simple good.
- Answering questions using short answers, refusing to provide details.
- Starts speaking more formally, this is an indication that the person is getting stressed.
- Exhibits lapses in their memory at critical times, despite the person being alert during an earlier interaction.
- Pay close attention to how the person says "No". No is a very vital word that you should observe is you suspect a person is trying to lie or mislead you.
- You should be aware of the very many compliments. Do not misunderstand me, there are sincerely nice people in the universe. But you should also watch out for people who try very hard to make a good impression.
- Consenting to all your views, continue offering praise and laughing at all the jokes you make are indications of a person who lacks sincerity and authenticity.
- Ask for the story backward. Sincere people will tend to add details and remember more truths as they repeat their experience. Contrary, Liars memorize their story and try as much as possible to keep them similar. When you suspect that a person is being deceptive, ask them to recall events backward rather than forward in time.

How to Overcome Deception

Deception has occurred to you, one time or another. You've put your trust in someone who did not deserve it and realized later that you were being deceived. Whether the deceiver was a family member, employee, business partner, spouse, or friend, you feel betrayed and hurt. Bet even worse, you feel responsible. "What is wrong with me I allowed this to occur? " you wonder.

Nothing, it turns out. If you have been taken for a ride by a qualified liar or a master in manipulation, all it means is that you are an honest person.

Tips to overcome deception:

- Do not give a known liar the benefit of doubt
- Learn and understand the basic elements of deception detection
- You should stop being shy about checking things out
- Do not change who you really are
- Always forgive yourself for being fooled.

Chapter 5: Brainwashing

This technique of mind control was first used in the 1950s during the Korean war. Brainwashing was applied to explain how the totalitarian regimes were able to complete the indoctrinate American troops via a process of propaganda and torture.

Brainwashing is the concept of a person's core affiliations, values, ideas, and beliefs are replaced, so much that the victims have no autonomy control over themselves and can't think independently or critically.

Who is Vulnerable to Brainwashing?

From the book of 'The Manchurian Candidate', a very prominent politician is held hostage by the Korean army during the war and the senator is brainwashed into becoming a sleeper special agent for the Korean military, with the intention of assassinating the presidential contender. From the book, you can learn that even the most intelligent and powerful many can be easily brainwashed, but in the truth, the opposite is very likely.

This includes people that have:

- Been forced to live on the streets
- Lost their loved ones via death or divorce
- Been made redundant or sacked from their workplace
- Suffered or are suffering from an illness that they can't accept

How a Person Can Be Brainwashed?

A person who is attempting to brainwash you will want to know every detail about your life in order for them to manipulate your beliefs. The person will want to find out what is your weakness, who you trust and what your strengths are, who is vital to you and who you listen to for advice.

After doing so, the person will begin the process of brainwashing which will involve five steps:

Isolation

This is the first tactic towards brainwashing because when you have family and friends around you is harmful to the manipulators. The last thing that they desire is someone with a different idea to their idea, asking questions about what you are being asked to believe. This technique begins in the form of not allowing you to access to friends or family or constant checking where someone is and who they are with.

Attack on Self-Esteem

When a person wants to brainwash someone, the manipulators can only do so if their target is in a vulnerable condition and has a low level of self-confidence. A person who is broken is much easy to rebuild with the manipulator's beliefs.

The manipulator requires to break down the target's self-esteem. This could be done through intimidation or embarrassment, physical abuse or verbal abuse, sleep deprivation. A manipulator will begin to regulate everything about the target's life, from the time they sleep to even using the washroom and from food.

Us Versus Them

For you to break down a person and reshape them in a different image, an alternative way of their livelihood must be introduced that is more attractive than the present livelihood.

Blind Obedience

This is the ultimate goal of a manipulator, where the target follows orders without question.

Chanting a similar statement over and over again is a good way of controlling a person. Not only is repeating the same statement a tip of calming the mind, but studies have shown that the analytical and the repetitive parts of the mind are not interchangeable. Meaning that you can only do one or the other, so how perfect to halt those doubting thoughts by chanting.

Monopolization of Perception

The abuser utter things that causes you to be introspective, you look deeper, to solve issues of your soul:

- The abuser keeps your attention on them.
- The manipulator makes it not possible for you to do things that are off-limits.
- The abusers try to remove anything from you would that they can't control.

Induced Exhaustion

Brainwashers tries to weaken your capability to resist their control by:

Finding tactics to make you feel guilty for not agreeing to their demands.

Keeping you often busy meeting their very high standards of holiness, parenting, and cleanliness.

- Claim your character is sub-par and they insist that you correct it.
- Demand that your friends with their boss's spouse, attend social events that improve their professional career.

- Add tasks to your life that are beyond and above what is often expected in a normal relationship.

Threats

The brainwasher threatens to leave you. The threats are credible to you. The abusers deliver the threats via body language too.

Degradation

The brainwasher harms you more when you resist their demands or question their ideas and stand up for your right. Any moment that your anger rises, the manipulator must deal with your fury, the punishment is more severe than if you just did the damn thing, to begin with.

The brainwasher will tend to degrade you with mere words, via physical or sexual abuse and humiliate you in the presence of their coworkers or friends at any time. The humiliation tears down your sense of self-worth to a lower level.

Demonstrate Omnipotence

Most Brainwashers will stalk you during relationships, use their friends or they will exploit lucky coincidence to prove that they know everything you do even when they are not present.

Testing

Brainwashers can never think of their work as accomplished, as there are often situations where the target could begin to regain control of their own autonomy and begin thinking critically for themselves again. Testing their targets not only shows that they are still brainwashed, but it allows the brainwasher to see just how much control he/she still has over his/her targets. The test could involve doing a criminal act, for example, burglarizing a home or robbing a store.

How to Heal from Brainwashing

Can you heal from and overcome brainwashing? Yes. So long as you know that you have experienced brainwashing, you will be able to heal from it and recover from domestic abuse and regain total control of your mind.

First, you should learn how your manipulator used brainwashing techniques to bring you under their control. Secondly, learn more about self-mind-control to undo the brainwashing.

Steps that you can follow:

- End Isolation. The fast method to get over any fear that you feel is to open up about the issue. It would be very wise for you to begin talking about your manipulation to a therapist. I know that not everyone is always ready for this, but you can start by talking about the weather or the last night's match, this will help you to gain some confidence first. Isolating yourself does not completely end the brainwashing by itself. You have to be around people who know about your abuse and who can serve as voices of reason in your surreal, brainwashed world.
- Learn more about various kinds of abuse. Knowledge is power, you can make use of it to rebuff your manipulator's attempts to humiliate and degrade you. You are less likely to feel worse about your manipulator's actions and words when you know that your abuser harms you to maintain control over you.
- Understand and learn as much as possible about domestic abuse and violence. Soon you will learn how to identify the kinds of verbal abuse your partner applies against you as they occur. By learning to identify the types of verbal abuse will give you the ability to detach from harmful behaviors and words because you will know specifically when your manipulator attempts to harm you. Get to learn what kind

of abuse is out there, and how they look like and sound like, and pay close attention to how the abuse makes you feel.

- A common question that you might have ever asked yourself is "Why does he/she abuse me!" Do not spend much of your time to research the answer to this question. The natural empathy may convince you that your brainwasher needs sympathy and that you can like them into mental health. Always remind yourself that abuse and brainwashing alter the definition of love. At this point you can't trust 'love' this is because brainwashing warped your perception of love - particularly when it's your abusive partner.
- Accept painful anxieties and thoughts. You will go through unpleasant feelings as you recover from brainwashing, you should deprogram your mind and leave your manipulator's world.
- As you accept that the manipulator is intending to harm you and their nice face is their mask, you will definitely experience fear. One of the most irrational and rational emotion is fear.

Stress Relief from Anxiety and Fear

One of the appropriate stress relievers for victims of manipulation is them leaving the manipulator. You will have more peace than you can ever imagine without that idiot breathing down your neck.

Most people are not ready to leave, maybe they have decided to stay there forever. Other ways that you can deal with anxiety and stress include:

- Listening to good music.
- Hypnosis for abuse victims.
- Deep breathing techniques.

- Proper nutrition.
- Meditation techniques.
- Better medical care.
- Having some spare time for some walk.

Chapter 6: Common Covert Manipulation Methods

Love Bombing

It is a process of grooming in which a manipulator applies praise, flattery, and the promise of a supreme alliance to fulfill their desires. By love bombing their subjects, manipulators are able to persuade their subjects to fulfill their desires and requests. It is not only a tactic applied by covert manipulators to exploit their subjects, but it is also applied in cults to make sure loyalty to the cult leaders. In fact, there is much overlap between the behavior of the cult and the abuse series of a manipulator and his/her subject.

While any person can be the subject of love bombing, it has a particularly powerful impact on kids of narcissistic parents or guardians, because they have already been subconsciously programmed to seek approval, engage in people-pleasing habits, and look for external approval as a way to survive their psychologically turbulent childhood.

Love bombing is an attempt to apply affection and attention to influence another person. The word originated from the Unification Church of the U.S.A, a religious organization with its roots in South Korea, who applied love bombing to convey sincere love and interest shown to other people.

According to many psychiatrists, the love bomb is applied as a weapon, a kind of psychological manipulation that is applied to maintain control and power in a relationship. Gang and pimps leaders apply the love bomb to encourage obedience and loyalty. Cult leaders have practiced love bombing to coerce followers into mass suicide. And many people apply love bombing to abuse romantic partners. It works because humans have a natural need to feel good about who you are, and usually you can't fill this need on your own.

At times the reason is situational, brought on by an event, like job loss or divorce. Sometimes it is more constant and traces back to your childhood. Whatever the source, love bombers are experts at spotting low self-esteem and exploiting it.

How to Identify Love Bombing?

It can be hard to tell the difference between an individual who is naturally affectionate and kind, and an individual who is applying such displays to manipulate.

How Do You Know If Love Bombing Is Occurring To You?

It is essential to recall that creating trust in a healthy relationship takes time. Love bombers want to rush the process, so they can get to taking advantage of unsuspecting subjects.

Unlike healthy relationship, that displays of affection continue indefinitely and actions match words, love bombing usually involves an abrupt shift in the kind of attention, from loving and affectionate to controlling and angry, with the pursuing partner making unreasonable demands.

A good litmus test for identifying a potential love bomber:

Think of your best ally, how much you have in common, and how often the two of you disagree or agree. Now consider how long it took to build that relationship. It is likely that someone you have just met knows you as well as your best ally? If you find yourself saying, 'Yes, they do!' warning bells should be ringing.

To protect yourself from falling into the trap of the love bomb, you should be aware of those who:

They are fast to show affection and warmth, but then lose their temper or find other ways to punish you when they do not get their way.

Constantly Seek to Stroke Your Ego

Push a relationship to limits that you are not ready for.

How can you prevent yourself if you suspect a loved bomber in your midst?

In the early stages of any relationship, do not fear to slow down when you feel that things are moving very fast. Limiting your personal contact and setting boundaries will keep you from falling under the subject's spell, and assist you to see your relationship from a more realistic perspective.

If you fear that you are already in an unhealthy relationship, attempt talking about it with trusted friends or family members or seek professional assistance.

Gaslighting

To gaslight, a person is to cause them to doubt something about themselves that is real. Though in a covert way, they tend to ask questions that would make think twice about even the things you have often held to be sacrosanct. For you to combat this emotional technique, you need to document your experiences and life happenings and you should often refer to them. This will help you not to doubt even a single of your experiences.

Denial

It's very hard to separate denial, lying and the distortion of facts from emotional manipulation. Although a manipulator may not often be opposed to the fact, their supposed acceptance of it is to serve their purpose to manipulate you later on. They will consent to a fact only to deny it later on. Projection Manipulators use this tactic to shift their shortcomings or deficiencies to another person. Instead of them taking responsibility for their errors, they would rather place the blame on someone else. It is an abusive technique that seeks to take the burden of guilt from them to another person. Their main purpose is to paint themselves clean while the other person looks unfortunate and dirty.

Chapter 7: Dark Persuasion

Persuasion is a form of mind control, it works to alter the beliefs and thoughts of the victim like the other forms of mind control. People will usually use persuasion to their advantage without them noticing. Persuasion changes the way that the victim is thinking. It can be found in your daily life and it is a very powerful force as well as a major influence on the victim and society. Compared to the other forms of mind control, persuasion can be performed on just one victim to change their mind, it's also possible to apply persuasion on a larger scale in order to persuade an entire group or society to change the way they are thinking. Hypnosis and brainwashing will require the victim to be in isolation in order to change their identity and minds. Persuasion is more effective and perhaps dangerous because it has the ability to change the minds of many people all at once rather than the mind of just a single target. Most people fall under the false impression that they are immune to the effects of persuasion. The act of persuasion is going to be very subtle and it can be very hard for the victim to form their own opinions about what they are being told.

Elements of Persuasion

These elements assist to define exactly what persuasion is so that it is more recognized. One thing that makes persuasion different from the other forms of mind control is that the victim is often allowed to make their own free decisions in the matter even if the techniques of persuasion are going to work to shift the subject's mind in a specific direction. These elements include:

It involves the agent deliberately trying to manipulate the victim or group is symbolic, it utilizes words, sounds, and images to get the point across self-persuasion is a vital aspect of this process. The victim is often not coerced and instead, they are given the freedom to choose their own decision. In order for you to persuade a person to think or act in a particular way, you need to be able to show them why they should alter their thoughts. For you to achieve this, you will include the use of images, words, and sounds to get your new point across. You can use words to trigger an argument to show your new point. Pictures can be a great way to show the evidence that is needed to persuade a person to go one way or the other. You will apply persuasion in a deliberate way in order to manipulate the ways other people think or act. The persuader will apply different tactics in order to get the victim to think the same way that they do. What is the difference between persuasion and dark persuasion? The difference between persuasion and dark persuasion is in the intention. A persuader might try to convince a person to do something without thinking through particular motivation or techniques or without any real understanding of the target they are attempting to persuade. A dark persuader often understands the bigger picture. The persuader understands who he/she is trying to persuade, what motivates them, and how far they need to take the technique in order for them to be successful. A dark persuader is typically unconcerned with the morality of his/her manipulation. He/she see doing the right thing as a perk, but it does not have to be his/her biggest motivation. In the Venn diagram of self-gratification and morality, dark persuader actions will not often fall into the overlapping section. A dark persuader will see the person or thing he/she wants and devise a way to get it by all means.

The Long Con

The confidence tactic begins with the basic human psychology

From the manipulator perspective, it is a question of recognizing the target; who is she, what does she desire, and how you can play on that need to accomplish what you want. It needs the building of rapport and empathy; an emotional base must be built prior to any plan is schemed. Only does the scheme move to persuasion and logic; the scheme, the evidence, and the way it will work to your advantage.

By the point where things start to seem dicey, you tend to get very invested, usually physically and emotionally that you perform most of the persuasion yourself. You may even choose to up your engagement, even when things turn south so that by the time you are completely fleeced, you do not know what hit you.

The manipulator may even not require to persuade you to stay silent; you are more likely than not to stay quiet yourself. You are the perfect deceiver of your mind. At every level of the tactic, manipulators get from an endless toolbox of techniques to manipulate your belief. Even as you get very committed, with every stage you give the manipulator more psychological material to operate with.

When it's a manipulator, everybody is a potential target. Despite your dew certainty in your immunity fall for it. The manipulator can persuade even the most discerning connoisseurs with their manipulative charm.

The Low-Ball Tactic

This tactic is applied mostly in sales instances to convince the customers to buy a product, and in some instances as a compliance gaining formula.

It is a compliance technique that is applied to convince someone to consent to an offer. Someone applying this tactic will present a very attractive request at first. The request will be very attractive for the other person to accept the offer. Then, prior to finalizing the deal, the person will change the deal.

The resulting offer will be less attractive than the initial request. Having committed to the deal, the other party will usually feel obliged to extend their compliance to the resulting offer.

Tactics involved in compliance:

- The door-in-the- face tactic as a compliance technique
- Ingratiation tactic
- Foot-in-the-door as a persuasive tactic
- The strategy is usually allied as a sale method. Sellers sell an item at a lower price, that their consumer consent to, then the seller increases the price of the same item before they finish the sale. Having already consented to the sale the customer reluctantly consents to the higher price.
- Low balling is a sequential offer strategy. Users of sequential offer make two or more similar offer. However, the users alter the terms of every offer, expecting their target to consent to the resulting question.

Requisites

For this strategy to be very effective, the initial request must be very attractive for someone to consent to it. The individual should give their consent to the request and be committed to it.

Why Does it Work?

As per the other sequential offer compliance techniques, the low ball depends on the sense of commitment that the other lesser request generates. Even as the terms of the offer changes, the target still feels obliged to be consistent in their character. The target feels that he/she should consent to the resulting offer so as to fulfill their other side of the bargain.

This strategy also depends on your urge for favorable self-presentation. Human beings often want to be seen in a positive way by their mates. People seek to preserve or gain a positive perspective on themselves. If the terms of an offer are altered, you are very reluctant to be viewed as fickle by avoiding to commit to the agreement and agree to the new terms as a tactic of maintaining your positive reputation.

The Law of State Transference

The natural capability to transfer a strong emotional state from one person to another.

It explains how emotions are contagious.

How Can Emotion Play a Role in Persuasion?

A neurologist Damasio Antonio carried out a study that shows the effect of emotions in the decision making the process. He studied people with brain damage that prevented them from experiencing feelings.

In the study they all acted in a natural manner, except for one issue, they were not able to make simple decisions. The victims could explain what they should be doing, logically speaking. Yet they all had a problem in making even the simplest decision.

Within the brain, there are two vital systems. System one is unconscious, automatic, fast, and low effort. System two is conscious, high effort, slow and controlled.

System one is your emotional processor while two is your logical rational processor.

The Elements of Emotional Persuasion

You will experience a wide variety of feelings in your life. All to a certain degree will impact your decision-making process.

There are some main feelings that everyone has a significant effect. They are feelings that system one is very familiar with. If you can appeal to these four feelings you can influence and persuade other people to decide.

They include:

- **Anxiety** - This is an unpleasant feeling characterized by an unpleasant state of inner turmoil, usually associated with anxious behaviors.

    How it influences decision making;

    - You will not be able this effectively interprets environmental context and cues.
    - You will be less confident in your decision-making process
    - You will be less ethical and more selfish

- **Anger** - Wrath or anger is an extreme emotional reaction. It is a natural emotion that consists of a firm emotional reaction and uncomfortable reaction to a perceived provocation. Usually, it shows when a person basic boundary is violated.

    o   How it influences decision making;
    o   You will feel empowered
    o   You will feel more positive and in control
    o   You will be able to identify a better judgment

- **Sadness** - It is an emotional pain related to or characterized by emotions of disadvantage, sorrow, helplessness, loss, and despair.

    o   How sadness influence decision making
    o   You will undervalue yourself and your possessions.
    o   You will make decisions based on short term gains.
    o   You will make decisions more slowly.

- **Awe** - It is a feeling comparable to wonder but a bit joyous. It is directed at objects to be nor powerful than the victim.

    o   How it impacts decision making
    o   You will be more giving. Those who experience awe are more giving of their time and are willing to assist other people.
    o   You will be present. When you experience a sense of awe, you at brought to the present. Your sense of time dissolves away and you get more concentrated than usual on what is occurring right now, at that exact time.

o   You will feel more satisfied. You will feel more satisfied with your accomplishments and status in life. In fact, you will feel more fulfilled and accomplished.

Chapter 8: Common Cons and the Dark psychology behind them

Embarrassment

Humiliation, guilt, shame, and embarrassment all suggest the presence of value systems, while guilt and shame are mainly as a result of self-appraisal, humiliation and embarrassment are mainly the results of appraisal by one or more people, even in imagination or thought.

One essential respect that humiliation differs from embarrassment is that, while you bring embarrassment upon yourself, humiliation is an aspect that is brought upon you by other people.

Another aspect of divergent between embarrassment and humiliation is that humiliation goes deeper. It is traumatic and usually hushed up, while embarrassment, given enough time, can sublime into a humorous anecdote.

More fundamentally, humiliation consists of the abasement of dignity and pride, with its loss of standing and status.

When you are just embarrassed, your status claims are not undermined, or if they are undermined, they can be easily restored. But if you are humiliated, your status claims are not easily restored, because, in this instance, your very own authority to your major status claim has been questioned.

Those who are in the process of being humiliated are often speechless and voiceless, and furthermore, they are stunned. When you are criticizing people, particularly those with low self-esteem, you must ensure that you do not attack their very authority to make the status claims.

Humiliation is a public failure of a person's status claim. The person's private failure amount not to humiliation but too painful self-realization. Potentially humiliating scenes ought to be kept very private.

Humiliation is stigmatizing. Humiliated people have the mark of their humiliation episodes, and are remembered and thought of by their humiliation.

Embarrassment is assumed as one of the two self-conscious feelings, very at ease in the company of pride, guilt, and shame. Given that embarrassment occurs in association with others, it is a public feeling that makes you feel filled with regret, awkward and exposed for whatever your wrongdoings are. Potential negative assessments concerning standards about behaviors, thoughts, and emotions that control your behavior are at the center of self-conscious feelings and embarrassment.

The feeling of embarrassment alerts you to your failure to act in compliance with specific social norms, which challenges the core beliefs which you hold about how other people judge you and how you assess yourself.

Embarrassment often is an outcome of accidental behaviors that make you feel negative about yourself, even if you have no intention of violating a given social standard.

Probably you would not take long to recall a unique embarrassment event, since embarrassment is often experienced, and, unfortunately, very well recalled.

Common human cues of embarrassment include:

- Face touching
- Head movements that turn away
- Downward gaze
- Smile controls

It's so curious why people have a peculiar smile with flatness and touch their eyes and corners of their lips show when they're embarrassed, but it's an embarrassment-related facial expression.

Embarrassment is related to blushing, however, not a person blushes upon being embarrassed. It happens when an emotional catalyst causes your glands to release adrenaline in your system, that causes your capillaries to widen.

It is quite interesting that in particular social events and circumstances, habits that would be ordinarily considered as embarrassing is taken as humorous and amusing.

A situation that causes humiliation is often thought to be the ones you'd be afraid of having a witness, so it seems paradoxical that you might feel embarrassed in some positive circumstances. For instance, if your boss recognizes your excellent performance and provides a large reward to you publicly, you can feel embarrassed rather than proud.

What Good is it, if it Makes You Feel Uncomfortable?

Embarrassment is likely to have developed to maintain social order because people feel ashamed to express that they accept and admit their wrongdoing and do better.

It has been studied that those who feel embarrassed at their social mistakes are more prone to be trusted, forgiven, and liked than people who do not and as an outcome, their embarrassment saves their face.

Embarrassment resembles the feeling of shame. Many humiliation elements are less intense shame associated with a negative self-assessment. Although shame and embarrassment are possibly related to some degree, the behaviors related to them involve distinct postures and facial expressions that differentiate them as emotions.

How to Handle Embarrassment?

Take a step back from your humiliation and just consider how it can affect the way you behave, how you socially active, and your general attitude to alleviate the condition in your mind over and over again. It will likely not be a positive impact. Clinging on to your embarrassing transgressions can decrease your self-esteem level and the way that you think of yourself. You are not your transgressions, but, instead, your mistake can assist you to grow and learn.

Dressing for Success

When it comes to judging other people, you perceive a broad variety of personal traits through your clothing preference. You jump to conclusions about values, professional competence, and viewpoints based at least on what you wear. Dressing for success exudes credibility and instills confidence.

Men Suited for Power Playing

Studies show that perfectly dressed people are so successful in negotiation settings. People in business suit achieve more from the perception of dominance. In a particular study, it was found that men in business suits showed dominance, measured by successful negotiations.

It was suggested that a self-fulfilling prophecy related to how wearing clothing symbolic of higher status can maximize self-confidence.

Role-Playing – We Are What We Put On

The reality is that what you wear impacts the way you act and feel. In a study known as unclothed cognition found that participants who wore tunics and associated them with nursing scrubs, felt more empathetic and demonstrated increased helping behavior than those who merely wore the scrub.

Nothing Like Provocatively Dressed Professional Ladies

In addition to demonstrating power and status, attire also influences the perception of competence. Relying on their position, ladies can lose the perception of competence by putting on provocative attire at work.

Suitability May Be in The Eye of The Observer

Various observers have different expectations of professional attire, and therefore they have different opinions about appropriate clothing. Professionalism is showed significantly via business grooming and dress.

Business casual clothing is preferred over casual clothing, although there is a preference for business clothing. Dark clothing is slightly preferred over lighter attire.

Style Influences Success

When you intentionally dress for success, you gain confidence through the way you are handled by other people, as well as how you perceive yourself. Strategizing professional clothing seems to be a wise way regardless of your field, and clothing induced achievement can be a self-fulfilling prophecy.

Appear Trustworthy

The benefits of projecting trustworthiness are significant, also the costs of failing to do so are enormous as well.

Employees are very willing to share some information with coworkers if they trust them. Most people are less territorial if they think of their colleagues as allies. Companies with the least turnover rates are those with leaders who inspire trust in their employees.

To find out if you are trustworthy or not, someone would analyze your deeds and words to know if you have good intentions toward him/her if you got what it takes to act on those intentions.

Someone's perception of you as being trustworthy, then, cheats in your capability to show competence and warmth.

There are tips that you can easily convey competence and warmth to other people:

Putting Your Perfect Face Forward

You could go straight out and tell a person, "I mean not to harm you," but because of the weirdness factor of saying such words, you'd be better off signaling you're warmth and competence more directly. The first step to doing this is indicating that you are paying close attention.

For you to achieve this, it is recommended that you smile, keep eye contact and nod to show that you are actually concentrating.

Maintaining eye contact indicates that you are actually listening.

Showing Empathy

Putting yourself in your perceiver's position and attempt to associate by figuring out a common experience, interest, and dislike.

An effective but usually overlooked technique is saying "I am sorry," You are not uttering this as a way to accept blame but to show your regret that something bad has occurred to your perceiver.

Trusting Others, Yourself

Humans are normally inclined to pay it forward, and reciprocity holds true when it comes to trust.

You are more likely to trust a person who has trusted you first, a person who is openly cooperative rather than competitive and put other people's desire above their own.

Demonstrating Striking Will Power

Would you place your trust on a colleague who has a serious self-control problem with an essential task? Probably No, if you publicly get involved in behaviors that indicate low will power, your trustworthiness will decline.

While a person's personal behavior would primarily remain personal, they suggest to outsiders whether or not the person can adhere to the set standards of any healthy relationship, that could involve those at your workplace.

To effectively show competence to your coworkers you either stop your negative habits or at least keep them to yourself.

Avoid Being Cocky

Anything that you do, do not mistake confidence with competence, whereas you cannot have too much competence, there is an unhealthy and healthy dose of confidence to know.

The harm of overconfidence includes butting off much than you can chew, being underprepared and mainly making poor decisions.

Instead, you should show a realistic feeling of confidence that indicates modesty. You will be less likely to threaten your coworkers' self-esteem, and your transgressions won't trigger nearly as many cheers from your cube mates.

Apply Body Language to You Benefit

An easier method to look more competent is by making eye contact as you speak. People who make eye contact while they speak are consistently judged as very intelligent.

Sitting upright, nodding, gesturing, and speaking faster all have been found to cause significant perception competence.

Standing with your arms on your hips is one of high-power poses.

By sitting and standing in an expensive way, you are not only indicating confidence to other people but also stimulating immediate alterations in your body chemistry that make you very powerful that goes hand in hand with competence.

Play on Your Greed

Greed is part of the dark personality trait or character flaws. Every person has the potential of having greedy tendencies but in those with deprivation or a strong fear of lack. It can be a dominant trait.

It is the tendency to selfish hoarding, craving, and grasping.

A selfish urge for more than what is deserved or required, particularly of wealth, food, money, and other possessions.

Components of Greed:

- A maladaptive tactic to protect self
- Misconception about the nature of the self, others, or life
- Early negatives experiences
- A constant sense of insecurity and fear.
- Greed in Action
- Compelling need

It is a compelling desire to consume, possess, or acquire more than is really justifiable or needed. You would feel this subjectively as an all-consuming desire, craving or hunger for a particular thing. This might be stimulated by suddenly seeing what you desire, or a chance to go after it. Underlying the urge, however, it is terrible insecurity, a primal depreciation or fear of lack, though it is likely to be unconscious than conscious.

Risky Commitment

If the urge is being firmly experienced, you get compelled to commit to a significant deal of energy and time to acquiring and seeking. The only perfect course of action is to attempt and satisfy the urge because it promises to give you that long-lost feeling of insecurity.

Other people might question your unique determination and commitment, given that it looks like you are willing to risk all over this personal peculiar obsession.

Brief Gratification

At times you may accomplish success in having what you desire. And in those times when the elusive thing of your urge is really in your hands, and your experience actually intoxicating emotions of relief and triumph.

However, that gratifying moment is too short, that you feel the win is merely enough. In fact, to you, there is nothing such as enough.

Despite all your best efforts, and all the success, an abiding feeling of fulfillment or security is never attained. The overwhelming urge is literally insatiable so long as the underlying emotion of fear is never dealt with.

Harsh Realities

You might thereafter feel frustration at the transience of this pleasure, particularly given the investment of energy and time.

You may face guilt and shame over the destructive impacts of your actions on your financial security, relationship, and reputation.

You may experience overwhelming anxiety over the unspecified future.

All these have the impact of triggering insecurity and fear, and a compelling desire to fill that empty hole, thus the cycle starts again.

You may face all these at the same time, or have those in your foreground at different periods. Still, it is quite comfortable to a series of addiction, in that the urge gets very difficult to satisfy, so the subject point of a fix or a win keeps increasing, that in turn needs more and more investment of money, energy and time.

There is a significant expense of self-esteem, as you get more enslaved to the urge. And a significant expense to a person's other commitment, that competes for the same energy and time.

Chapter 9: Micro Expressions and Body Language

Understanding Body Language

Most of you have some intuitive understanding of body language that you develop over the countless social interactions that you take part in during your life. However, having a deeper understanding of nonverbal cues can assist you to read a person, read a room or even pick up on potential threats. One perfect way to apply body language is, to begin with, someone's face and work your way down, doing a mental checklist. What is a facial expression like? What are they doing with their hands? How are they sitting or standing?

Understanding body language can assist you to ensure that you are sending the correct message out in the universe. When you want to look friendly and open, you do not stand and sit in a closed position.

If you are worried about your incapability to understand body language, social cues, and facial expressions, consider visiting a counselor.

Micro Expression and their Interpretation Micro expression is a facial expression that happens fast and dissolves away. A microexpression is involuntary and indicates a person's emotional response for a specific moment. A microexpression is difficult to fake, micro expression happens very fast, often in about 1/15 to 1/25 a second, faking microexpression is not possible. It may be very hard to identify micro expression unless you are staring at them. Below are micro-expressions and their potential meaning:

One part of the mouth drawn up - hate

Lips smile with corners up, wrinkles with cheeks pulled up in the corner of the mouth, wrinkles show from the jaw down to the corner of the lip-happiness.

The inner corner of the eyebrows pulled in and the outer side down, the inner corner of the ears pulled up, and the skin taut, the corners of the lips pulled up, the jaws pulled up, and the lower lip juts out into a pout-sad.

Wrinkles in the middle of the forehead, eyebrows up and straight over, upper eyelid lifted with lower taut of the eyes, white visible above the iris not below open the mouth and the lips pulled back and taunted-fear

Eyebrows arched and raised, skin taut on lower eyelids, wrinkled forehead, white of the eyes visible below and above the iris, jaw open teeth parted - surprise.

Vertical wrinkles between the eyebrows, eyebrows pulled and taunted together in the center, lower eyelid tense and focused, lips draw tight and the corners down, lower jaw slightly forward - aggression, anger.

The upper lid of two eyes and lower lip is raised, the nose wrinkles and cheeks raised - response to something disgust, smelly.

Nonverbal Cues Associated with Sitting

You spend a lot of time, particularly your social time when nonverbal cues are most essential, sitting down. How you are sitting can tell a lot about your feelings and attitudes in a particular situation:

81

Knees Apart

A popular thread that you will see in this section is that the larger a person seems, the more confident they are likely to feel or want to appear.

If someone stands or sits in a way that makes them appear larger, they may be attempting to boost or intimidating to other people. Any of these can be the instance for sitting with the knees apart. Sitting with the knees apart makes someone look larger and it also makes them appear in charge, relaxed and comfortable. Therefore, confident. This is primarily a more masculine posture and it would be more popular to see a man sitting in this posture than a woman.

Knees Together

Just as a person is sitting with their knees apart can look larger, therefore, more confident, a person sitting with their knees together can look smaller and is likely to be on the edge or worried. This is because sitting with knees together is a closed position that indicates that someone is attempting to protect themselves. Sitting with knees together is not particularly seen as a feminine posture in the way that sitting with knees apart is seen as a masculine posture.

Knees Crossed

Sitting with knees crossed often has a deeper meaning than simply sitting with the knees together. It makes someone appear quite small. It can be seen as a closed and defensive posture and unlike sitting with knees together, is often seen as an explicitly feminine posture. It is considered polite and dainty. It can indicate discomfort or shyness.

Ankles Crossed Under Knees

Sitting on the floor with your ankles crossed and the feet under the knees is usually seen as a sign of thoughtfulness and comfort.

Names of this pose vary in place and time. In the Pacific region, it is usually called lotus posture and is displayed in both ancient and modern illustrations of thinkers and holy men and is believed to have been adopted as one of the most comfortable postures for long term meditation.

Nonverbal Cues While Standing

How you stand can also tell you a significant deal of how a person is feeling or thinking:

Feet Apart

Having your feet apart makes you appear larger and is a more stable stance. As a result, it is usually seen as being comfortable, confident, and potentially aggressive.

Feet Together

Standing with your feet together makes you appear small and so is often held by those who are less comfortable. It is also usually a sign of respect as when soldiers standing at attention.

Slouched or Supported

Standing while supported as with a foot or the back against the wall indicates not aggression or comfort. It is at times seen as being disrespectful or that the person is not paying attention to the interaction around them.

Arms in The Pocket or At the Sides

Standing with your hands at the sides, depending on their stiffness, is sort of neutral position. Stiff hands and straights shoulders are often reserved for signs of respect as is the instance with soldiers standing at attention.

However, standings with arms in your pocket are usually seen as disrespectful in particular events. It can be viewed as distracting and there is room to assume that the person is more preoccupied with whatever is in their pockets that with what is going on.

Hands Crossed

Standing with your arms folded on your chest makes your body seem smaller and is a closed posture. It can be a sign of discomfort, and anger. Having your hands crossed over your chest is often seen disrespectful, possibly because it can be viewed as creating a barrier between you and the other person, indicating disapproval or disinterest.

Hands Up

Having your hands raised is usually seen as a sign of submission. In conflict, people who have surrendered usually have their hands raised as a sign that they are not reaching or holding for a weapon.

Palms Together

Holding your palms together can mean several things depending on the context but is very often a contemplative gesture. It is usually performed while thinking but is usually performed while praying. Directing the thoughts to heaven.

Holding your palms together specific in the pacific zones, in practices like yoga, it symbolizes balance. The pose is symmetrical with the palms meeting at the center of the body.

Arms Behind Your Back

Standing with your arms behind your back is often a sign of patience, contemplation, and comfort. In the armed services and martial arts, is usually sewn a semi-formal stance.

Touch

You are involved in touching routinely and it includes patting a person on the back or granting the person a hug to indicate that you care. You commonly shake hands as greetings or assign to signal shared understanding. Touch as a form of communication is called haptics. For kids, touch is a vital aspect of their development. Kids that do not get enough touch have developmental problems. Touch assists babies to cope with stress. At infancy, touch is the first feeling that an infant respond to.

Functional Touch

At the workplace, touch is among effective means of communication but it is necessary to follow the popular rules of etiquette. For instance, a handshake is a kind of touch that is used in the professional field and can show the relationship between two people. Pay close attention to the nonverbal signs that you are conveying next time you shake a person's hand. Generally, you should often convey confidence when shaking another person's hand but you should avoid being overly-confident. Praise and encouragement are communicated by a pat on the shoulder. You should recall that not all people share similar comfort levels when using touch as nonverbal communication. For instance, an innocent touch can make another person feel uneasy and for this reason, using touch needs reading the body language and responding effectively.

Additionally, at the place of work, touch can get complicated when it is between a subordinate and a boss. Standard practice is that people in power are not allowed to touch their subordinates than vice versa. For this reason, you should evaluate your motives for the most trivial of touches and decide to enhance your communication tactics with your juniors. A standard measure is that it is better to fail but on the side of caution. Functional touch includes being physically examined by a doctor and being touch as a form of professional massage.

Social Touch

Most types of communication need some kind of touch. A handshake is an essential touch in social touches. Handshakes vary from culture to culture. It is polite socially and allowed for one to shake another person's hand during an introduction in the United States. In other countries, kissing on the cheek is the culture. In the same interactions, men will allow a male stranger to touch them on their arms and shoulders, whereas women feel comfortable being touched by a female stranger only on the arms. Men are likely to enjoy touch from a female stranger while women tend to feel uncomfortable with any touch by a male stranger.

Friendship Touch

The types of touches allowed between allies vary depending on contexts. For instance, women are very receptive touching female friends compared to their male counterparts. The touches between female friends are very affectionate often in a way of a hug whereas men prefer to shake their hands and pat one other on the back. Within a family setting, female touch each other compared to male.

Displays of affection between friends are critical in expressing encouragement and support even if you are not a touchy person. One should be willing to get out of their comfort zone and offer their friend a hug when he or she is in a difficult situation. Helping others enliven their moods is likely to uplift your moods as well.

Intimacy Touch

In romantic relationships, touches that communicate love play a critical role. For instance, the simplest of touches can convey a critical meaning such as holding arms or placing your hand around your significant other which communicates that both of you are one. Adults pay attention to nonverbal signs compared to verbal cues during an interaction.

In the earlier moments of dating, men tend to start the physical contact in line with societal norms but at a later point of the dating, it is women that touch first. Women place more premiums on touch compared to men and even the smallest of gestures can help calm women they were upset.

Arousal Touch

Arousing touches are elicited intense feelings and are only suitable if mutually agreed upon. Arousal touches are for evoking pleasure and happiness and can involve kissing, flirtatious touching, and hugging that is intentional to suggest sex. One should be careful about their partners' needs. One can greatly improve their communication skills and relationships by paying close attention to the nonverbal signs that you convey to other people via touching habits.

Additionally, our sense of touch is intended to communicate clearly and quickly. Touch can elicit subconscious communication. For instance, you instantly pull away from your hand when touching something hot even before you consciously process. In this manner, touch constitutes one of the quickest ways to communicate. Touch as a form of nonverbal communication is an instinctive form of communication. In detail, touch conveys information instantly and causes a guttural reaction. Completely withholding touch will communicate the wrong messages without your realization.

Chapter 10: Undetected Mind Control

Undetected mind control is the most deadly form of mind control in existence. When a person is aware that their mind is being influenced then they are able to object physically, mentally, or verbally. They are able to avoid contact with the controlling situation or person. Many people would run at the first sign of a harmful individual attempting to get inside their mind and take control over it. If their mind controller is undetected, like a stealth bomber, then it is impossible for the subject to put their defenses up in time.

The use of media and interpersonal interactions. Traditionally, media mind control was only possible for large companies and individual mind controllers were left to interpersonal mind control.

Nowadays this is no longer the occasion. Smartphones and computers have placed media mind control powers directly into the hands of the coldest manipulators in the universe.

Undetected Mind Control Techniques

Media Mind Control with Sound

You love to think that you have a free will, and the decisions that you make and the thoughts that you have are your own. Your feeling of individuality, free choice, and identity are part of what makes you special and play an integral part of the human experience. Yet you are actually as possessed and independent of free will as you would love to think?

The very thought that you could be under the influence of outside subjects and forces to manipulation by mind-control against your own will is a horrible aspect that has been explored deeply in science fiction, but what if it is not just fiction at all?

What if you are directly programmed and shaped by nefarious people via the TV you watch daily and the music that you listen to routinely? According to others, this is really what is occurring, and has been there for years.

A technology that can be applied to subliminally influence you and reach out over the airwaves is known as the Silent Sound Spread Spectrum (SSSS).

This technology was created in the 1950s and perfected over the years and it operates by analyzing the human mind patterns and then storing this data as emotion signature cluster, that can be beamed, duplicated, and synthesized via different medium so as to subliminally influence the emotional thought process and states of humans, particularly disrupting your consciousness.

It is a very silent communication system that has non-aural carriers, in the very high or very low audio frequency range or in the next ultrasonic frequency spectrum are frequency, or amplitude modulated with the wanted intelligence and propagated vibrationally, or acoustically for introduction into the mind, primarily via the application of earphones or loudspeakers, or piezoelectric transducers.

The modulated carriers are sent directly in the real-time or maybe appropriately stored and recorded on optical, magnetic, or mechanical media for delayed, or repeated transmission to the person listening.

Covert Mind Control

The main tactics that the technology is utilized are either via application of piggybacking or short-range direct microwave induction on the signal sent over the radio or TV waves and other carrier frequencies. This is supposedly entirely undetectable.

So creepy, particularly looking at the potential military application for such a technology.

Media Mind Control with Images

It looks that it is a popular first response. The fact is a lot more disturbing and subtle. Mass media has long been applying different mind control tactics to trigger the worst in you.

It is a formula of applying knowledge by the elite people to control the masses but with no physical external force. The elite people, however, require your permission to accept their dark agenda, and there are some ways in which the elite do it:

- The elite distract you
- The elite make you feel bad about yourself
- The elite dumb you down
- The elite use fake news
- The elite numbs you to violence.

The giant media cooperation makes a decision on what commercial adverts you view in-between programs and also have a significant influence on what new programmers get commissioned or remain on the air. Their influence is widespread and encompassing.

At the beginning when you want to watch TV, you are in your natural beta brainwave state. However, after a few minutes, you go into what is called an alpha brainwave state. This is a relaxed condition of the brain that feels peaceful. The more you watch, the more this condition continues and maximizes.

The issue is that the alpha brainwave state makes you more susceptible to what you are watching. It lowers your feeling of cynicism and leaves you feeling receptive to what you are watching. It is like a hypnotic state where you are susceptible to whatever is being shown to you.

When you change from a beta state to an alpha brainwave state, you get incredibly relaxed. This is a quite pleasurable and powerful feeling. It can get very addictive and is one of the factors that most people love to relax by getting a couch potato.

How is it even possible for the media to apply mind control methods, below are some of the ways they do it:

Criminal TV Shows

How do they numb you to violence?
By showing intense violence in criminal TV shows and justifying it by offering it a storyline. Early exposure to violence on TV causes aggressive behavior in future life.

Advertising

Everywhere you look in advertisements on TV, billboards or magazines, there are images of perfect people selling a product. Of course, you don't expect advertisers to apply ugly models, in modern decades, the stakes in advertising have been raised to an impossible beauty standard.

There is no possible way that the ordinary citizen can keep up with what is being promoted and advertised as normal beauty.

Chapter 11: Mind Games with Dark Psychology

The mind game is a kind of social impact that aims to alter behaviors or ideas through underhand, abusive, or fraudulent tactics. By maximizing manipulative interest, usually at other expenses, these tactics may be considered deceptive, exploitable, confusing, and insulting.

Social impact is not necessarily negative. For instance, people like allies, family, and doctors can clearly agree to change rude behavior. The social effect is primarily considered to be depleted when it respects the right to reject or accept and is not unreasonably compulsory. Relying on the motivation and context, the social effect may involve underhanded manipulation.

You are playing mind games because it makes you feel secure and avoid taking responsibility for your emotions. The challenging part of playing mind games is that you never have an actual relationship with humans and thus do not feel a deep love connection that comes from belief and honesty.

Below are general mind games:

Forget Passive-Aggressive Personality

Basically, such people forget essential issues such as debt repayment, recruitment, and commitment. You wait for them to recall, but they do not, and when you remind them, they reply, 'Oh, I am sorry, I forgot'. After getting it many times, you begin to get bored. Then they reply, 'Oh, I am actually sorry, are you upset? You feel upset.' When you are upset with them, they protest, 'Oh, God, I would have told you.' By doing that you are not upset about anything, that makes you even more upset. In this manner, they suppress your anger without giving them the chance to express your anger.

Offense

Tripping here the game is done in such a manner that if any person wants to perform their work, they feel guilty.

Incompatibility

It is a way to say something harmful to a person, and thereafter, when they get hurt, it seems hesitant that what you mean is not really right.

Torture

At times people hate their projects and oppression towards other people. They are either known about their hate, or they think it's fair. Once they begin the project, they look for the reasons for torture. When hateful people disagree with them in politics, reject invitations or laugh at the wrong way, then the persecutors find ways to punish them. They could talk trash about them behind their backs or might speak with them in an insulting or condescending manner.

Shaming

People who play the mind game, see their anger when they catch people who do not like to say something that is not inappropriate. This is the opposite of a personal ideology; it is demonizing any person.

Playing Hard To Get

It applies when women and men intentionally attempt not to show their affection and interest for the person they are dating. The aim is to make themselves look more valuable in the eyes of their date. They do not want to look desperate or easy.

Guilt-Tripping

People use this tactic to make others weaken their personal boundaries. An individual who feels guilty will usually allow other people to walk over them and do things they would not do if guilt was not there in the first place.

Love Bombing

It is what manipulative people usually do at the start of the relationship. They attempt their best to look like the perfect, wonderful lover from your own rather than a natural individual. They may buy you gift all the time or even text you constantly and move the relationship fast. It is essential to differentiate between normal showing/flirting and love bombing affection. Love bombing tends to be more intense than natural flirting and seems way less inappropriate and realistic for the stage of the relationship.

Testing Limits

This is when someone intentionally does something disrespectful or hurtful to you so that to test your response and your boundaries. They want to see if you are a person with weak boundaries or if you can stand up for yourself. Those who do this are primarily people who are looking for a person with weak personal boundaries and that is why they try to test your boundaries.

Gaslighting

It is a manipulation technique that manipulators apply to make their subject question their own reality. What they do is that they withhold information, they lie to your face about trivial matters, they deny they ever said something you recall they said to confuse you, they accuse you of being overly forgetful or crazy. They may even hide or misplace your items to make you question your memory.

Reasons Why People Play Mind Games

People who apply mind games often because they are immature, insecure or have a manipulative kind of personality. They are not ready and mature enough to be in a stable personal relationship. Most of this stems from personal insecurities and the inability to connect and trust with others in a healthy manner.

To manipulate - Most people apply mind games that they selfishly manipulate other people so that they are able to have what they desire to meet their own unmet desires. This may include:

- Having a person to listen to them
- Hoping someone will heal their deepest hurts.
- Strengthening their self-image because they have an identity to present to others.
- A need to control a person
- Having a person to adore them
- Sex
- Often have a person by their side.

People like the thrill-some people just want to see if they can get them to like a girl or a boy. It's like a race or a match for them. They say to themselves, if I can make a guy or a girl like me, then I must be really cool. All this emanates from an unawareness of how they hurt other people and low self-esteem. Others are in a frantic brain condition, needing the satisfaction of feeling that they matter for at least one man.

Testing the waters-in an attempt to figure out how you feel about them, many people play mind games. To be honest enough to share your deepest desires to want to love and be loved takes so much bravery. What if you're telling a person that you're actually taking care of them and that in some way you're referencing ten.

You may feel like being led on, but maybe the other party is just anxious about making the first move.

How to Play Mind Games?

Since in time memorial, people have been applying manipulative techniques to get other people to say or do particular things. You must be able to trick people without making your intentions known to you in order to play mind games. You will find yourself manipulating other people's emotions and thoughts by learning specific techniques and fine-tuning your acting skills.

Method 1: Becoming Convincing to Other People

Sign up For an Acting Class - When learning how to trick a person, it is essential that you learn how to make that person believe in your emotions and words. Learning basics acting tactics can assist you to get more persuasive to people you are trying to manipulate.

Don't Break Your Character - When a person calls your bluff or accuses you of trying to mess with their mind, do not admit it. It is possible to turn the situation around, and convince that person that their accusations or paranoia hurt your emotions:

- When you admit that you are playing mind games, you will low that person's trust.
- Be charming-people are more receptive to those who are charming, and they are more inclined to trust them;
- Often have a smile, have a welcoming body language, and treat every person with equality and respect.

Become Charismatic - People tend to reply positively to people who make them feel happy and special. Charismatic people are perfect at doing because they possess particular values. Below are some methods you can apply:

- Give compliments
- Reply to their emotions to show that you really care
- Ask about their interests.
- Say people's name when you part ways or greet.
- Make eye contact during an interaction.
- Show confidence-show others that you value yourself and they should too. This lets others be more likely to listen to what you have to say and you.

Be Seemingly Vulnerable - If you share your sensitive side and deep feelings, it makes people believe there is no room in your personality for deception. You want people to think you are being transparent and have nothing to hide;

- Express your admiration for pretty things or gracious acts
- Be empathic

Method 2: Understanding Those Around You

Studying other manipulators - when you find out another person has been practicing mind games on you, or a person you know, and has done it well, find out what made them successful. Understand their words and mannerisms to find out their tactic.

Practice analyzing people-be sure to analyze the person you are attempting to play mind games on so that you understand how that person thinks. This will let you take the perfect approach for getting this person to engage in your mental game.

Watch for emotionally driven people-many people are easily responsive to emotional hardships and situations. For empathetic and sympathetic people, you will want to play to their feelings by having them feel bad for you. This will lead them into assisting you however you say you require it.

Playing the victim-this technique needs that you gain the sympathy of the person. You require to act like you are a perfect, moral person who keeps being victimized by the evils of the universe, and you just do not understand why. This will make the person feel obligated to give in to any request you may have.

Looking for guilt-ridden individuals-if you know that a person is sensitive to guilt, be sure to play on that weakness. Guilt can weigh heavily on a lot of people, and they will do their best to avoid that feeling. If you go to ask for a favor that person may not want to do, you can try to guilt trip that person into performing it. Below are some statements that you may say if a person turns you down;

- "I am not surprised that you won't do it, I am used to it."
- "I knew you would let me down."

Method 3: Sending Mixed Signs to a Significant Other

Don't reply immediately to phone calls and texts - those who are often available leave little room for deception and mystery. Instead of waiting by the phone to engage in an interaction, allow him to think that you are busy;

- If he calls you, do not reply it. Call him back hours later, or maybe even the next day. Your unavailability will leave him guessing.
- If he texts you in the morning with a flirty greeting, do not reply back until hours later. This will leave him wondering where you are and who you might be with at that particular time.

Being Flirtatious Around Others - If it is just the two of you hanging out, allow the sparks fly. Show him that you two have perfect chemistry, and something special may come out of the relationship. Then, when you two come around others, show some flirtatious attention to other ladies. This will really mess with his mind.

Disappear for Some Days - Maybe you have been spending a lot of time together, and things seem to be heating up. Throw him off course by not speaking to him for some days;

When he texts or calls, asking you to meet up or just chat, simply and him a text that explains that you are busy. Be vague and tell him that you will text him in a few days when you get an opportunity.

Say That You Are Fine When You Are Not - When your partner somehow disappoints you or let you down, tell him that everything is okay and you understand, but then act angry. This will really play games with his mind.

Method 4: Controlling the Feelings of Other People

Testing Your Dignity - Some people do not like to claim defeat, or admit when something becomes challenging for them to perform. By presenting undesirable tasks in particular ways, you can easily convince a person to consent to what you desire.

Show That You Care - When you show a person that you care about their well-being, or you desire to have him/her as an ally, it will normally invite that person into your life;

Figure out a way to assist a person out, and after completing the task, ask for a favor. It will be difficult for that person to turn you down.

Do a person a favor. If you go out of your way for another person, that person will feel indebted to you and will desire to return the favor.

Instill Fear and Thereafter Provide Relief - A perfect way to influence the way a person makes a decision, is to make them fear a situation enough to be willing to do whatever you say to avoid it from occurring;

When you want a person to begin exercising with you, give statistics about how not working out can cause terrible health issues. Thereafter, explain how you can teach them great exercise to avoid getting those health issues.

Figuring out a person's desire - when you are dealing with people who are driven by desire, simply explain an easy way to get what they desire. Tell them how to easily make more money, but a better vehicle, or get a job promotion. Making the person believe that they can have a brighter future by doing what you say is an easy way to play mind games.

Chapter 12: Applications of Dark Triad

Psychopathic Actions

Psychopaths are not capable of feeling empathy, guilt, or remorse for their actions. Psychopaths are primarily manipulative and cunning. Psychopaths understand the difference between wrong and right but they do not believe that those rules apply to them.

The First Interaction with a Psychopath

On the first impression, they primarily seem reasonable, caring, logical, friendly, and charming, with a well-thought-out desire. Psychopaths give the impression that they are able to reason logically, that they understand the results for unlawful and antisocial behaviors and will respond accordingly.

Psychopaths seem able to self-examination and are able to criticize themselves for their mistakes.

Under clinical assessment, they do not indicate common symptoms related to neurotic behavior; mood swings, nervousness, extreme fatigue, high anxiety, headaches, and hysteria. In events that most natural people find upsetting, they look void of fear and anxiety and they appear calm.

An About-face

Initially, they look trustworthy, devoted, and reliable, but, suddenly and with no provocation, they get unreliable, without regard for how their actions impact the event, regardless of its importance. Once viewed as sincere and honest, psychopaths do a sudden about-face and start lying without consideration, even in small issues when there is no benefit in lying.

Because they have understood and mastered that art of deception, people around them are quite slow to accept the abrupt change. If they are confronted with their irresponsibility, lack of loyalty or honesty, it primarily has no effect on their future performance or attitude. Psychopaths are not able to perceive that others value integrity and truthfulness.

Cannot accept Responsibility for Failure

They change into performers who are able to mimic natural human feelings that they have never experienced. This holds fact if psychopaths are faced with episodes of failure. When psychopaths look to be very humble and take responsibility for their mistakes, their true aim is to be seen as the martyr or sacrificial lamb willing to accept blame.

When the scheme fails and they are blamed, psychopaths will emphatically avoid any responsibilities and with no shame, turn to finger-pointing, manipulation, and lies.

If they cannot persuade other people that they are not guilty, psychopaths obsess, and fume over it, usually murmuring sarcastic comments and planning revenge.

Risky Behavior with No Gain

Antisocial habit; stealing, committing adultery, cheating, agitating, robbing, killing, stealing appeals to them, whether or not they get any rewards. Psychopaths look drawn to a high-risk antisocial habit that has no clear aim. Experts theorize that they love to put themselves into harmful events because of the adrenaline rush they have. Because they primarily don't experience many feelings that natural people feel, any chronic feeling feels good. Other people believe that psychopaths do it to instill their feeling of superiority and to prove that they are smarter than others.

Horrible Judgment

Although they are logical thinkers and see themselves as very intelligent, psychopaths consistently show bad judgment. When faced with two paths, one to gold and the other path to ashes, they will take the latter. This is because they cannot learn from their experience; psychopaths are prone to taking a similar path again and again.

Unable to Love and Egocentric

They are very egomaniacal, to an extent where a normal human being has challenges understanding it. Their aspect of being self-centeredness is very deeply rooted that it makes them not capable of loving, including their own children, spouses, and parents.

The only time that they express an ordinary reaction to special treatment or kindness by other people is when it can be applied to their benefit. For instance, a psychopathic mother still loved by the kids despite the suffering she has caused the kids may put on a show of appreciation so that they continue to put money into her prison account or paying the legal fees.

Conventional Treatment Empowers Psychopaths

Some studies show that there are no conventional techniques to cure these habits. If conventional procedures have been applied, they get empowered and respond by enhancing their cunning and manipulative tactics and their capability to hide their true personality.

Difference Between Sociopaths and Psychopaths

Sociopaths and psychopaths have a common diagnosis of having an antisocial personality disorder and similar traits but there are great differences. Psychopaths are very manipulative and deceptive and maintain control over their external personas. Psychopaths can lead what seem to be normal lives, at times throughout their life. If they become criminals, they believe that they are invincible and smarter than the average person.

Sociopaths usually allow their anger surface with violent episodes, physically and verbally. Sociopaths get spontaneous and reckless and have a bit of control over what they say or how they behave. Because sociopaths are impulse motived, they rarely consider the outcome of their behavior. It is challenging for sociopaths to live a natural life, and because of their imprudence, most of them drop out of school, cannot hold jobs for long, turn to crime and eventually end up in prison.

Who is Very Dangerous?

Sociopaths gave a hard time concealing their disorder, while psychopaths pride themselves on their manipulative capabilities. Psychopaths are masters of dissociation and less likely to feel remorse or guilt for their behaviors. Because of this, psychopaths are considered to be very dangerous compared to sociopaths.

Narcissistic Actions

In the context of psychology, habits can be explained as being covert or overt. Overt habits are those which can be easily seen by other people, like those of the traditional narcissist. Covert habits, however, are those that are less obvious and more subtle to other people.

An introverted narcissist is a person who craves importance, and admiration as well as lacks empathy towards other people but can behave in a different manner than an overt narcissist.

When considering the actions of a narcissist, it may be challenging to think about how a person could be narcissist and be inhibited in their behavior and approach. An introverted narcissist might be externally withdrawn or self-effacing in their approach, but the ultimate aim is similar. This might be explained as listening to your favorite music while blasting the volume, compared to listening to a similar song on a low volume. The music itself has not altered, just the volume that you are listening.

Covert vs. Overt

A covert narcissist is only different from the overt narcissist in that they are more introverted. The overt narcissist is easily recognized because they are insensitive, arrogant, and loud to the desires of other people and often lust for compliments. Overt actions can be observed easily by other people and show up as big in the room.

If you think of an overt narcissist, you could say they show more extroverted actions in their social interactions with other people.

Both overt and covert narcissist go through the universe with a feeling of self-importance and fantasizing about grandeur and success.

Both require to meet similar clinical criteria to be diagnosed with a narcissistic personality disorder, whether they are introverted or extroverted. Both individuals have deficits in their ability to control their self-esteem.

Most people have fallen subject to the manipulate behavior of an introvert narcissist without them knowing what has occurred until they are already in emotional pain. It might be very accurate to assume that the overt narcissist would be much easier to see approaching than the introverted narcissist.

Signs to Look For

Although there are various clinical criteria that require to be achieved so that a person can be diagnosed with a narcissistic personality disorder, there are various primary traits and patterns to check in daily interactions when you suspect you might be handling an introverted narcissist. Be aware of these common traits they can assist empower people who are interacting with an introverted narcissist, assist them to identify and better go through potentially unhealthy interactions:

Passive Self-Importance

The covert narcissist will be more obvious in the elevated feeling of their arrogance and self when interacting with other people, the introverted narcissist may be less obvious. The introverted narcissist certainly desires importance and craves admiration but it can appear different to people around them. They might give back-handed compliment, or purposefully decrease their talents or achievement so that others will provide them with the reassurance of how talented they are.

In reality, both the covert and overt narcissist is that they have a very fragile sense of self.

The overt extroverted narcissist will command for attention and admiration, where the introverted narcissist will apply softer techniques to meet those similar aims. The introverted narcissist will be more likely to constantly seek reassurance about their accomplishments, skills, and talents looking for other people to feed that similar need for self-importance.

Shaming and Blaming

Shaming other people is a terrific technique for the narcissist so that to protect their feeling of an elevated position in association with other people. The overt narcissist may be very obvious in their procedure to gaining leverage, like explicitly putting a person down, being sarcastic, being rude and criticizing.
The covert narcissist may have a gentle method to explain why something is your mistake and they are not to take the blame. They might pretend to be a subject of your action to put themselves in a position to get reassurance and praise from you. Ultimately, the main aim of these interactions is to make the other party feel small.

Creating Confusion

Often not a sneaky, most introverted narcissist can take happiness in generating confusion for a person they are interacting with. They may not interact in shaming or blaming, but instead, causing others to question their perception and second guess themselves. Also, to generate leverage between them and another person, the introverted narcissist requires applying techniques like this to maintain power and elevate themselves in an interaction. If they are able to get you to question your perception, then this let them the chance to exploit and manipulate you more.

Disregard and Procrastination

Because their desire for self-importance is superior, an introverted narcissist will perform anything they require to do so that to keep the concentration on themselves. So, where an overt narcissist will blatantly manipulate you or push you aside to achieve their desire, the introverted narcissist is a professional at not acknowledging you at all.

It is not a coincidence that narcissists, in general, tend to gravitate toward interacting with compassionate and caring people. The introverted narcissist identifies those chances for manipulation too. They have no difficulties letting you understand that you are not essential.

Emotionally Neglectful

They are inept at creating and growing an emotional relationship with other people. How can they understand how to nurture bonds with other people if their energy and time are often concentrated on themselves? The introverted narcissist is not different. Although they may seem less obnoxious and kinder than the overt narcissist, they are not emotionally responsive or accessible too.

You will likely not get many compliments from an introverted narcissist. Recalling that they are often concentrated on staying elevated to maintain their feeling of self-importance, it is easier to know how an introverted narcissist would find it challenging to compliment you. There is often less regard for your abilities or talents.

What to Do

You may be in a personal relationship with an introverted narcissist, whether a coworker, significant other or a family member. It may be meaningful to note that although you can't manage what the narcissist does, you can regulate how you are interacting and behaving with them around. There are particular tips that you can take to secure yourself if having to deal with an introverted narcissist.

Don't Take it Personally

If you are dealing with a narcissist person, whether introverted or extroverted narcissist, their manipulative habit can be quite personal. The lack of patterns of manipulation, sense of entitlement, deceptive behaviors and regard behaviors of a narcissist can be personal if you are on the receiving side of their actions. No matter how painful the effect of the actions of a narcissist might be in the moment, it is essential to recall that it has nothing to do with you.

Setting Boundaries

They do not have strong boundaries. This is because the introverted narcissist has no empathy feeling, have a strong feeling of entitlement and exploit other people, boundaries are something that gets in the way of their desires. The more you can practice setting boundaries with the narcissist, the more consistently you are showing them that their techniques are not working on you.

Machiavellian Actions

Machiavellianism involves cynical and manipulative views, deceit toward human nature and cold, calculating moods towards other people.

A Cold, Calculating Opinion of Other People

Machiavellians are very strategic people who are more willing to deceive, cheat and lie to other people so that to accomplish their desires. Because of inadequate emotional attachment, and shallow experience of emotions, there may be less that holds these people back from hurting other people so that to accomplish their desires. This, in fact, is one of the factors why Machiavellian attitudes and views are so problematic and aversive. Indeed, similar these psychopaths who may hurt other people for enjoyment, or narcissists who may harm others because they lack empathy, they may deceive or manipulate other people so that to advance their self, with little concern of the emotional collateral.

Hot Empathy and Cold Empathy

A difference has been made between a feeling of empathy that is cold and cognitive and a feeling of empathy that is hot and emotional. Particularly, cold empathy means your knowledge of how other people are thinking, how other people react to specific events, and how situations may occur involving particular people.

An Evolutionary Advantage

While some Machiavellian express deficits in hot empathy, other Machiavellian have a perfect capability to know the feelings and emotions of other people, yet do not care. Particularly, a group of Machiavellians has been discovered to bypass the feeling of empathy; they have a perfect knowledge of the feelings and thoughts that may occur in other people as a result of manipulation, lies, yet fail to control their reaction. This inadequate of moral conscience in Machiavellian has been viewed by evolution psychologists as evolutionary advantageous in the aspect that these people may not be held back by a concern of other people, in pursuit of their desires. The question comes concerning how they can maintain and develop a firm emotionally satisfying relationship with other people if they lack the capability to emotionally resonate, or simply have a bit of consideration for the feelings and thoughts of other people.

Theory of Mind

It is the capability to appreciate and understand why people think in the unique manner they do. It differs from empathy, in that it more broadly refers to the contents, desires, aspirations, and goals within a person's brain, rather than their moment-to-moment alterations in feeling and thinking. They must have a reasonably perfect theory of mind so that they can know what motivates the actions of other people so that they are able to persuade these other people. However, Machiavellianism is negatively related to social cooperative techniques and theory of the mind; that assumes that these people may not be very successful in manipulating and understanding other people as they claim to be. Thus, while the character of Machiavellianism may consist of a set of attitudes and beliefs about manipulating other people, it is not a must that this manipulation technique will succeed.

Alexithymia

Machiavellianism is related to alexithymia that explains a deficit in understanding and naming a person's feelings. Those who are alexithymia have been defined as aloof and cold, and out of touch with their emotional experience. Alexithymia in Machiavellians may be as a result of a decreased understanding of feelings, which emanates from a shallow experience of these feelings or deficits in theory of mind and empathy. Regardless of the root cause, evidence shows that they are people who are more cognitive in their procedure towards themselves and other people, and who are out of touch with their feelings generally.

Chapter 13: Dark Psychological Seduction

Seduction is an art of psychology, and not beauty, seduction is within the grasp of any individual to be a master of psychological seduction. All you need is to look at the universe differently, via the eyes of a seducer.

What seduces a person is the effort that you expend on their behalf, show how much you care, and how much you are worth.

They take pleasure in performing, and they aren't weighed down by their try identity, or be natural, or desire to be themselves.

It has two aspects that you need to understand and analyze: first, yourself as a person and what is seductive about you and secondly, your actions and target that will go past their defenses and make them surrender.

Types of Seducer Targets

A piece of advice, do not try to seduce your own type. Most people constantly give out signals of what they don't have; you must tune in to these signals and interpret your type based on the signals.

- **The Beauty:** They are used to being appreciated, you must concentrate on the less complimented aspects like her wit or intellect.
- **The Rescuer:** people who desire to feel like they are saving someone from themselves.
- **The Professor:** They think deeply and analyze everything, but they desire to be more overwhelmed by a free spirit who can assist them release their mental obstacle.

- **The Aging Baby:** they are still immature and want a supportive parent, you have to enable their childish goals while still reel them in.
- **The Sensualist:** people who are driven by their senses, you have to overwhelm their touch, smell, and sight, to completely reel them in.
- **The Floating Gender:** Float with them.
- **The Roué:** They are more experienced, and their desire is to educate someone who is naive.
- **The Lonely Leader:** they act as their superior or equal, the type of relationship they don't have.
- **The Idol Worshippers:** You have to become their object of worship that gives a meaning in life that they desire.

Seductive Character

It begins with who you are, that is, your personality and the kind of seductive energy you expend. It needs refining yourself, building yourself in one of the following seducer categories:

- **Sirens** - They have plenty of sexual energy, and they know how to make use of it
- **Rakes** - They insatiably adore the opposite, and their urge is infectious.

Seducers lure their victims, just like the sirens of Odysseus, via their teases and image. Coming up with the appropriate seductive pose for their prey.

If there is no obstacle that you are facing, you must create the obstacles. Seduction thrives through obstacles.

Perfect lovers have an aesthetic sense that they use for romancing

Successful seducer in history was the Casanova, his technique was quite simple: on meeting a lady he would carefully study her, get along with her moods, find out what is it that she is missing in her life, and he would provide it instantly.

Dandies love playing with their own image, creating an androgynous and striking allure.

Do you feel more trapped within the limited roles that the universe expects you to perform? You are likely to be attracted to people who are very ambitious, more fluid, than you are - those who build their own persona.

Dandies often seduce socially and sexually: groups form around the Dandies, their unique style is mostly imitated, an entire population will fall in love with the Dandies. For you to adapt to the Dandy's character for your own benefits, always remember that the Dandy is naturally beautiful and a rare flower.

Naturals

- They are open and spontaneous
- Self-esteem is important in seduction. Having a low level of self-esteem repels, confidence and self-sufficiency attract. The less you may seem to need others, the more likely they will be attracted to you.

Charmers

- They tend to want and know how to please others, they are social creatures. They don't fight or argue, pester, or complain.
- Charismatics have unusual self-confidence in themselves, creating an air of charisma.
- You should learn to build the charismatic illusion by radiating more intensity while you remain detached.
- People don't want to hear that your success and power comes from years of discipline and effort. They prefer to

think that your power and success comes from your character, your personality, which you were naturally born with it.

The Brute

- They have no patience, they want to skip the seduction aspect, and they offend with egotism.

The Suffocation

- They are people who cling to you incessantly; they love you even before you know who they are, or those who make themselves a doormat to you in their obsession.

Seduction Phase 1: Separation, Desire, and Stirring Interest

- Choose the perfect target.
- The perfect targets are those people whom you can fill a void, those who see in you something exotic
- Leave those who are not accessible to you alone: you can't seduce everyone.
- Never be in a hurry to run into the waiting open arms of the first person who seems to like you. That isn't seduction but insecurity.
- Those who are outwardly distant are always perfect victims than extroverts.
- You should avoid those who are preoccupied with work or business – seduction is all about attention, and people who are busy have little time to spare in their routine for you.
- Once you have decided on the appropriate target, you have to stir their desire and get their attention. To move from friendship to love
- Your friendly interactions with your victim will give you access to very valuable information about their

weaknesses, tastes, characters, the childhood yearnings that regulate their adult behavior. When you spend time with your target you make them feel more comfortable with you. You should then, surprise your target's expectations with an errant touch that makes them more interested in you.

- There is nothing effective in seduction as making the seduced feel that they are the ones doing the seducing.
- Too much attention will suggest insecurity and raise doubts as to your motive.
- In every aspect of your life, you should not give the first impression that you are desiring for something, this will raise a resistance that you will never lower.
- Send different signals
- That which is striking and very obvious may attract their attention, but that attention will not last for long: finally, ambiguity is much more potent.

Seduction Phase 2: Lead Astray

- Create confusion and pleasure
- Keep your target in suspense?
- Behave in a manner that leaves your target wondering. Performing something that they don't expect gives them a sense of spontaneity - they won't be able to see what is coming next.
- Reliability is key for reeling others in, but you should stay very reliable and stay a bore. Dogs are very reliable, seducers are not.
- Make use of the power of words to plant confusion in them.
- Inflame other people's emotions with heavy phrases, flatter your targets with sweet words and not only will

they listen to you, but they will lose their will to resist you anytime.

- Pay close attention to details
- Poeticize your presence.
- Disarm through strategic vulnerability and weakness
- The appropriate way to hide your track is to ensure that the other person feels stronger and superior.
- Confuse reality and desire – the perfect illusion
- A seducer to bring some blood and flesh into a person's fantasy life by embodying a fantasy figure, or building an event resembling that person's dream.
- Separate the victims from their environment mentally, physically, and emotionally, so that the victims can become further engrossed with you.

Seduction Phase 3: The precipice, deepening the influence via extreme measures

- You should prove yourself.
- Don't worry when you make a mistake
- Cleverly and sneaky lead your target into chaos, a moment of danger and you can play the rescuer, the brave knight
- Stir up the taboo and transgressive
- Effect the regression.
- Make your victim feel that you are leading them past their kind of limit, this is extremely seductive.
- Make use of spiritual lures.
- Mix pain with pleasure
- Lure your victim with focused attention, then alter direction, appearing not interested anymore. Make your victim feel insecure and guilty.
- Ensure that your seduction methods should never follow a simple course upward towards harmony and pleasure.

This will ensure that the climax doesn't come too soon, and the pleasure will be too weak.

- With no suspense, tension, and anxiety, there can be no feeling of release, true joy, and pleasure. It's your responsibility to create tension in the victim; to trigger feelings of anxiety, to lead them to and from, so as the climax of the seduction has the actual intensity and weight.

Seduction Phase 4: Moving in for the kill

- Give the victim some time to fall, the pursuer is pursued
- You should stir up the pot by tending to be interested in someone else. Make some of this too explicit: allow your victim to only sense it and their imagination will perform the remaining, building the doubt you want.
- Understand: an individual's will power is directly associated with their libido, their erotic urge. When your target is passively waiting for you, their erotic level is very low and vice versa.
- While you're cool, the pantyhose air is calming the minds of your victim and lowering their inhibitions, bearing, voice and your glances. Getting under their skin, raising their temperature, and agitating their senses

Use Physical Lures

Be aware and alert to the signs of physical excitement. Trembling of their voice, unusual forceful laughter, blushing - these are signals that your target is slipping into the moment and pressure is to be used.

- Beware of the after-effects.
- Maintain your lightness and mystery.
- Be a master of the art of bold move.

- One of you must go on the offensive, and that should be you.

Avoid slow burnout. Immediately you feel disenchanted and know it's over, end it fast with no apology, and there is no going back.

Chapter 14: Case Studies of Dark Psychology

Ted Bundy - Final Testimony

Who Was Ted Bundy?

In his later confessions, Ted said he engaged in necrophilia and that he shampooed the hair of one victim and applied makeup to another victim, both postmortem.

One of the most notorious serial murderers in America, Ted was known for charming his young female subjects into complacency before brutally assaulting and murdering the victims. Though Ted Bundy murdered at least thirty women, Ted went relatively unnoticed until August 16, 1975, when a routine traffic stop led to the discovery of multiple suspicious items, including pantyhose, handcuffs, an ice pick. He soon became a suspect in murders across the United States, and his eventual trial in June 1979 was the first to ever be televised nationally in the United States.

Ted was born on November 24, 1946, in Burlington, Vermont, at a used mother's home. His mother was twenty-two years old Eleanor Cowell, and to this day, the identity of the father has never been known. Growing up, Ted lives in Philadelphia with his grandparents and aunts, whom he used to believe were his parents.

As a child, Ted appeared fully normal - for the most part. According to the investigative journalist Sullivan Kevin, there is one point from Ted's childhood that foreshadowed his future as a serial killer.

In 1950, Ted and his birth mother shifted to Tacoma, Washington, where she married a man called Culpeper Bundy Johnnie, who adopted young Ted. They went on to have four kids of their own. Ted said he grew up with two loving and dedicated parents in a Christian home with no physical abuse, drinking, fighting, smoking, and gambling.

But during his teenage, Ted became enamored by detective magazines that were full of stories of extreme crime and how to get away with it. A psychologist who assessed Ted said that Ted experienced much of sexual relieving through the fictional stories. Ted also disclosed in later interviews that his exposure to these magazines led to him seeking out violent pornography and more potent, more explicit, more graphic type of material.

Around this period, Ted was twice arrested on suspicion of auto theft and burglary, but the details of both cases were expunged from his record when Ted turned 18 years. Aside from these minor run-ins with the law, Ted was described as a good-looking socializer, by his high school friends.

After graduating from high school in 1965, Ted drifted between different colleges before enrolling at the University of Washington. A shy student, Ted was insecure about his lower-middle-class upbringing and believes he had nothing to offer his peers. But in 1967, Ted met a fellow University of Washington student. She had grown up in a successful, wealthy family in California, which Ted desperately wanted to be part of. The two dated for less than a year, and then she broke off the relationship because she believed Ted was directionless and unsure of himself.

Ted was devastated by the break-up and her rejection was a huge blow to Ted's ego. Many people believed that her rebuff may have stimulated Ted's murder spree and possibly motivated him to target women who looked similar to her.

In 1969, Ted seemed to have moved on and begun dating a new lady, who was a young mother and divorcee. Along with hanging out and taking classes with his new girlfriend, Ted became involved in politics and volunteered for Republican presidential nominee Rockefeller Nelson. He also worked at the Seattle suicide prevention hotline, where he worked and met with Rule Anne, a former police officer, and aspiring crime writer.

In 1979, Ted graduated from the University of Washington, making the honor roll. He was then accepted into law school at the University of Puget Sound.

First Murders

Continuing in politics, Ted worked on the committee for the Republican Governor J. Evans George re-election campaign. Ted was tasked with keeping tabs on Evan's opponent, and he posed as a college student and shadowed him to gather Intel. When Evans won the election, Ted was appointed as the special assistant for state Republican Chairman Davis Ross.

In the summer of 1973, Tedd went on a business trip to California for the Washington Republican Party. Though still in a relationship with his new girlfriend, he reached out to his college girlfriend, who had broken his heart. She was surprised at the changes Ted had made after their breakup.
Impressed by the new Bundy, his college sweetheart was joyful to rekindle their relationship, and he stopped responding to her letters and calls. One month later, she finally got ahold of Ted. She asked why he had suddenly stopped their relationship, and he very calmly replied, "I have no idea what you mean." That was the last time they spoke.

She came to the realization that Ted had planned this rejection from the start of their renewed relationship. Ted had waited all these years to be in a position where he could make her fall in love with had m, just so that he could drop her, reject her, as she had rejected him.

Back in Seattle, Ted had dropped out of law school and was working as the assistant director of the Seattle Crime Prevention Advisory. While working there, Ted wrote a rape-prevention pamphlet for women.

Though it was debated when Ted started killing, Ted carried out the first killing that police can conclusively attribute to him in 1974, shortly after his breakup with his college sweetheart. On January 4, Ted broke into the apartment of eighteen years old University of Washington student Karen Sparks.

Ted beat her close to death with a metal rod, which he also used to sexually assault her. She survived with permanent disabilities.

Less than one month later, he broke into the basement apartment of another University of Washington student, twenty-one-year-old Ann Healy Lynda, whom he beat, abducted, and murdered. On March 12, 1974, nineteen-year-old Manson Donna Gail left her Evergreen State College dorm room to attend a campus jazz concert when Ted abducted and murdered her.

Ted's fourth victim was eighteen-year-old Central Washington University student Rancourt Susan to his Volkswagen beetle by pitting on a sling and asking her for assistance moving some books. Two female Central Washington students later came forward to report that they had also been approached by a man calling himself Ted.

Ted's Later Murders

On July 4, 1974, Ted approached 23-year-old Ott Janice at Lake Sammamish State Park. Ted apparently asked for assistance unloading a sailboat from his Volkswagen beetle, as his arm was in a sling. Ted then abducted and murdered her. Hours later, Ted came up to nineteen-year-old Naslund Denise in the parking lot, again wearing a sling and asked for assistance. She was never seen again.

According to multiple witnesses, both Naslund and Ott were seen talking with a man who identified himself as Ted. As news of the Washington disappearance spread, police released composite details and sketch of the suspect, including a description of his car.

At this point, Ted had found a new job, working at the State Department of Emergency Services. Ted's coworkers had mixed emotions towards him. Some liked him while others thought that he was a manipulator and a slacker. Usually, Ted would not show up for work and didn't bother to tell his managers.

When police announced the disappearance of Naslund and Ott, Ted's colleague teased him unmercifully. The head of Rescue and Search group also joked about Bundy being a look-alike for the 'Ted' the police were looking for.

While they had no idea, Bundy was really responsible for the murders, four other people close to Bundy reported him to the police as a possible suspect. His girlfriend and a Professor from the University of Washington all knew a person called Ted who matched the composite sketch and drove a tan Volkswagen beetle. Although Bundy was being looked at by the police, he seems so natural that he didn't actually seem like the kind of person who would be a vicious killer. Bundy was never questioned by the police.

In August of 1974, Ted moved to Salt Lake City to attend the University of Utah law school. From his new house in Salt Lake City, Ted began murdering again in the fall of 1974. On October 28, Bundy abducted, strangled, and raped seventeen-year-old Smith Melissa, the daughter of a chief of police in Utah.

Bundy's First Arrest

On August 26, 1975, a Utah Highway patrol captain noticed a suspicious vehicle in a Salt Lake City suburb. When the Volkswagen beetle sped off, the offer game chase before the driver stopped at an empty gas station.

The officer said that the driver identified himself as a second-year law school student at the University of Utah. He said he was lost in the subdivision. He acted normal. The officer could not smell any beer, or alcohol on his breath. He was a good-looking young man. There was nothing to indicate anything was wrong.

Ted gave the police permission to search the car, and inside the police found a ski mask, handcuffs, pantyhose, ice pick, and a crowbar.

Bundy was arrested for suspicion of evading. Utah police were aware of the serial murders in Washington and had noticed Bundy was from Seattle. They were able to get a sketch of the suspect in the murders and realized it looked quite similar to DaRoch's description of her attacker. Bundy's movement also matched up with the timeline of the disappearance and murders, and the female victim all fit the same profile.

All the victims were in their late teens and had a similar physical description. The bodies were recovered were all naked and most showed signs of mutilation, trauma, sexual assault, and blunt force.

Bundy was placed under surveillance, and in September, Utah detectives went to Seattle to interview Ted's girlfriend, who had called the police for a second time after women began to disappear in Utah.

On October 2, 1975, DahRoch picked Busy out of a line and he was arrested for kidnapping. In February 1976, Bundy was found guilty and sentenced to one to fifteen years. Throughout the entire trial, Bundy maintained his innocence and denied his connection to the other murders and abduction. Because of had s background, appearance, and upbringing, most people could not believe the young paw student was responsible for the brutal murders.

Soon after his kidnapping conviction, however, detectives were able to charge Bundy with murder. Thanks to the several gas receipts and hair evidence taken from Bundy's impounded Volkswagen beetle, he was charged with the slaying of twenty-three-year-old Campbell Caryn, who was murdered in Colorado in 1975 January. Bundy was extradited to facility in Aspen for his murder trial.

Florida Murders and Escapes

Bundy represented himself throughout the trial, and to adequately prepare for his own defense, Bundy was granted special privileges by the court. Bundy charmed everyone he came into contact with and was given a telephone credit card, law books with access to the law library and health foods. During the trial period, he was allowed to take off his leg irons and manacles.

On June 7, 1977, he went up the law library during recess. With the guard outside the library door, he jumped out the open second-story window and escaped. He injured his ankle during the jump, but he was able to hike the Aspen Mountain.
Even the Aspen town was not immune to Bundy's charm.

Days after making it up the Asen Mountain, he stole a vehicle and tried to flee the town. But due to the broken ankle, Bundy drove erratically and was pulled over during a routine traffic stop. Bundy was taken back into custody immediately. He was placed in an isolated, maximum-security cell. Though there was a small hole in the ceiling from a light fixture that required welding, no one at the jail believed anyone would be able this escape through the small hole.

While incarcerated, he experienced a dramatic weight loss, that the other prisoners in their cells heard Bundy crawling up above them in the ceiling at night. He entered the jailers' apartment above the cells and put on civilian attires before escaping.

Now on the FBI's most-wanted list, Bundy made his way south, eventually settling in Tallahassee, Florida. Bundy checked into a boarding housing under the name Hangen Chris. Early morning of January 15, 1978, He entered the Chi Omega sorority house of Florida State University. With a wood log, he beat and sexually assaulted four ladies.

Capture and Florida trials

On February 15, 1978, He was pulled over another routine traffic stop. When pulled over by the police, he resisted arrest and attempted to flee on foot. After giving them a fake identity, the cops didn't know who they had in custody. After some days, he was interviewed and introduced himself as Robert Bundy Theodore. Bundy was charged with Florida homicides and assaults.

A pre-trial was arranged where Bundy would plead guilty to the charges for a life sentence of 75 years without parole. At the pre-trial, He refused the deal, and the case went to trial. In June 1979,

Bundy's trial became the first ever to be broadcasted on national TV in the United States.

Even though Bundy did not finish law school, he was again allowed to represent himself, and the judge appointed him a co-counsel. Bundy was found guilty of murdering both Bowman Levy and Margaret, three counts of attempted murder and two counts of burglary. He was sentenced to death.

Death and Confession

While awaiting his execution date, he gave a series of interviews, most notably with FBI profiler Hagmaier Bill. For three years Bundy never admitted to any of the murders. Bundy would talk about his crimes in the third person and refer to some unidentified serial killer.

Later, he tried to stretch out his time before sent to the electric chair. Bundy wanted to come clean about who he killed, how he killed them and where their bodies were located.

During Bundy's death-row confessions, Bundy admitted that he was involved in at least thirty homicides between the years 1973-1978 across seven states.
Bundy also opened about his motivations behind the murders, saying, murder is not just a crime of lust or violence. It gets to be part of you. It gets to be your possession. You feel the last bit of breath leaving their bodies. You are looking into their eyes. A person in that situation is God!

He revealed that he would usually revisit his subjects after they had been killed. The fresher the find, the more likely he would be back.
Bundy told Hagmaier, "If you have got time, they can be anyone you want them to be."

Bundy admitted taking photographs of his victims, explaining, if you work hard to do something right, you don't want to forget it. The night before his execution, he talked with Hagmaier about committing suicide, He didn't want the government to be happy to watch him die.

At 7:26 AM on the morning of Tuesday, January 24, 1989, Bundy Ted was pronounced dead after being electrocuted at Florida State Prison. While being strapped he told his lawyers to give his love to his family and friends.

Truths and Myths About Rasputin

The death and life of Rasputin Grigory Effimovich are filled in mythology, making Rasputin an almost larger than life personality in Russian history. A political saboteur, renegade monk, sexual deviant, and mystic healer, the mysterious Rasputin was revered and reviled during his life and became a scapegoat for some dissident group of the decade.

Take a look at the truths and myths about the legendary Siberian holy man:

Mystical Powers

He was born to peasants in a village in western Siberia, the young Rasputin turned to religion early in his childhood. Even as a kid, rumors were that young Rasputin had specific mystical powers. Despite fathering several kids, he abandoned family life in search of Orthodox Christian religious piety and devotion. After years of religious teaching and years of wandering, he ended up in St. Petersburg, the seat of royal power. Through some connections, he became popular with Nicholas Tsar and his spouse, the Alexandra Tsarina.

Desperate to get a cure for their sick son's hemophilia, one night they called upon Rasputin. After the session with the boy, the bleeding seemed to halt for a while.

Historians, like, Galliard, have suggested that hemophilia likely stopped because of Rasputin's insistence of not allowing the administration of aspirin; aspirin is known as a blood-thinning element, and not any mystical powers Rasputin may have had. The Tsarina was happy, and immediately enlisted the services of Rasputin as a close personal adviser.

Rasputin Was a Sexual Deviant and the Queen's Lover

Stories of Rasputin's sexual behaviors started to spread with time within the royal court, as his eccentric habit, like visiting brothels, and heavy drinking was viewed to collude with Rasputin religious piety.

According to historians who believe that Rasputin may have been a faithful member of, or influenced by the great Khlyst religious cult, such a sinful habit brought him closer to Almighty. However, though Rasputin did frequently entertain in salons, there was no evidence suggesting Rasputin was a sex-crazed maniac who had a secret relationship with Russian's queen.

Much like all his life, Rasputin's character in this aspect has been exaggerated and following the February 1917 revolution, embellished by his foes in attempts to propagandize his life.

Rasputin Was Russia's Secret Ruler

Due to his consistent appearance in the Royal court, whispers were that he was acting as a puppet master over the royal spouse. Alexandra's constant dependence on him and Rasputin's apparent healing capabilities with her hemophiliac son only exacerbated these whispers.

Occasionally, the Rasputin did give military advice as well as medical help, but his opinions did not prove beneficial for the Russian military or Nicholas Tsar. In fact, after Nicholas took personal charge over his military on August 23, 1915, under the counsel of Rasputin and Alexandra, Nicholas became the subject of blame for Russia's military defeats. Meanwhile, with Nicholas away in battle, a vacuum of power was filled by the Tsarina. Here, the myth approaches the fact. Though the Tsarina was in charge, Rasputin did have significant powers as her personal adviser. Rasputin wasted no time in appointing his own church ministers and other public officials.

Rasputin Was Impossible to Kill

His influence and habits came to represent everything negative in Russian society and politics at that moment. Even before his final assassination attempt, other assassination attempts on his life were carried out. In June 1914, a beggar lady stabbed Rasputin in the stomach, claiming Rasputin was seducing the innocent beggar. He made a complete recovery, even though Rasputin had lost much blood and was near death after the stabbing.

Two years later, a section of nobles led by Felix Yusupov planned to kill Rasputin once and for all. On December 30, 1916, Felix invited the monk to have dinner at his home. After a very heavy meal, full of dessert and wine, all with heavy laced poison, the section of noblemen looked on, as amazingly, he showed no signs that the poison was affecting him. The noblemen then proceeded to shoot Rasputin, who, according to tales still drew breath after a barrage of bullets and only died after he was thrown into an ice-cold river to drawn.
However, while his death was in fact planned by Felix and other noblemen, the autopsy report suggested that no poison was found in his system.

Rasputin Rose From the Dead

Much like the story of his murder, the aftermath of his death has been mythologized over the decades. According to a tale, after his poisoned and shot body thrown into the ice-cold river, he was fished out by a group of passers-by, who found that Rasputin was still alive when they dragged his body to the shores of the river. It took the police days to find the body because in the sub-zero Russian winter the water had already frozen.

But the myths about His survived, and some reality remains below those myths. Some historians claimed that the power of Rasputin actually played a role in the disdain of the royal family and all that it came to represent. Rasputin's tale actually showed that mythology could lead a life of its own and become more important than the truth.

Conclusion

Thank you for making it through to the end of Dark Psychology let us hope it was informative and able to provide you with all of the tools you need to achieve your goals whatever they may be. If you are ignorant of the tactics applied to you by the manipulators, you will not be able to break loose from their spell. You will always deceive yourself that you are in charge of your life when you are really not in charge of your life. When you have the ability to identify the tactics used by the manipulators, you can easily identify when they are being used on you.

The condition that causes shame is often thought to be those you'd be afraid of having a witness, so it seems paradoxical that you might feel embarrassed in some positive circumstances. For example, you can feel embarrassed rather than feeling pride when your employer recognizes your excellent performance and publicly rewards you with a substantial bonus.

Finally, if you found this book useful in any way, an honest review is always appreciated!